When Leadership Mattered

Inspiring Stories of 12 People Who Changed
The World

By Baxter Ennis

DEDICATION

This book is dedicated to those who strive mightily to fight evil and right wrongs, who make us better by their demand for excellence, quality, and justice—each one "who is actually in the arena, whose face is marred by dust and sweat and blood" (Theodore Roosevelt). They demonstrate not just courage but grit and tenacity and refuse to quit even when success seems impossible. They are never satisfied with the status quo. They are ordinary people who do extraordinary things. They change our world.

When Leadership Mattered

CONTENTS

INTRODUCTION

As someone who has a lifelong passion for history, I have always been fascinated by the stories of leaders—men and women who challenged the inevitable and changed the status quo, leaving their imprint on the world.

This book was not written to be a groundbreaking treatise or scholarly work about the twelve people featured in this work. For most of them, their lives and achievements have been well documented.

What I have sought to do is to produce short biographical sketches about certain periods in the lives of these remarkable leaders that the average person with limited time and energy can pick up and read and maybe learn a few things. I have sought to focus on those "moments of destiny" when their leadership mattered.

I strongly encourage you to do additional reading and studying about any of the people mentioned in this book. They have fascinating stories—many things we were never taught in school.

Anyone attempting to change, improve, or build something in a new way will face opposition and adversity at some point. These twelve certainly did. But there is a great story of perseverance and tenacity in each that should inspire us all.

My desire is that you come away from reading this book knowing that one person can make a difference! Whether it's in a battle, government service, fighting for rights, coaching a team, or leading your business, one leader can change everything!

CHAPTER ONE

Patrick Henry

On May 29, 1765, one unknown young man spoke up and changed the world!

There are times when things are a mess! It might seem your business, your city, maybe even your nation is on the verge of calamity, and no one seems to know how to prevent it.

This was the case in the spring of 1765 when Virginia's House of Burgesses in Williamsburg had, without a fight it seemed, acquiesced and allowed a loathsome bill, the Stamp Act, to be enacted by the British crown in London.

The Stamp Act required a government stamp (or tax) on every publication, some 55 specified items ranging from legal documents to newspapers and even to playing cards. The purpose of the tax was to fund the stationing of 10,000 troops to defend the vast new frontier territory that had been won during the French and Indian War.

Young Patrick Henry had arrived in Williamsburg on May 20, appointed to fill a vacant seat in the House of Burgesses. Being new to the Assembly, he restrained himself from speaking as the wise and powerful members of the assembly, men like Peyton Randolph, Edmund Pendleton, Thomas Jefferson, and John Robinson (speaker of the House for 30 years) discussed the Act, grumbled about it, but, to his disappointment, offered no plan to fight its enactment. The respected grand old men of the Assembly had given up the fight on the Stamp Act, and it was scheduled to go into effect November 1.

However, on May 29, his 29th birthday—and only nine days after taking his seat in the Assembly—Henry, indignant at this royal power grab, rose to present his Stamp Act Resolves. He delivered a spellbinding speech against the Stamp Act and turned the assembly on its head!

One of his Resolves defiantly stated, "…the General Assembly of this colony has the only . . . exclusive right and power to lay taxes . . . upon the inhabitants of this colony." [1]

A heated debate ensued. Henry, backed by George Johnston and John Fleming, defended his Resolves against the powerful men of the aristocracy: Randolph, Bland, Pendleton, and others. For two days the debate raged. During this debate Henry's fiery and impassioned oratorical skills were showcased for the first time.

Some of the most contentious remarks made by Henry during the debate led this speech to be known as his "treason speech." He said:

> "Caesar has his Brutus; Charles the First his Cromwell; and George the Third. . ." [Then he is interrupted] "Treason," shouted the Speaker. "Treason, treason," rose from all sides of the room. The orator [Henry] paused in stately defiance till these rude exclamations were ended and then, rearing himself with a look and bearing of still prouder and fiercer determination, he so closed the sentence as to baffle his accusers, without the least flinching from his own position, "and if this be treason,

---

[1] Patrick Henry , qtd. in William Wirt Henry, *Patrick Henry: Life, Correspondence and Speeches* (1891; reprint, Harrisonburg, VA: Sprinkle Publications, 1993), pp. 80-81.

make the most of it."[2]

According to Judge Paul Carrington, Henry was "eloquent" and his oratory "beyond his powers of description."[3] Finally, the Resolutions objecting to the Stamp Act were passed, and, although the House of Burgesses later defeated the most extreme of Henry's resolutions, four of the seven Resolves were adopted.

Patrick Henry speaking before the Virginia Assembly.

Providentially, copies of the original Resolves were leaked to the public, and some or all of the Resolves were printed in several prominent northern newspapers. Word spread to the other colonies like wildfire. The spark of rebellion had been ignited!

Because of his courage and passion for moral government, Patrick Henry's Stamp Act Resolves emboldened leaders in other colonies to adopt similar resolutions. By November 1, 1775, the implementation date of the Stamp Act, every stamp distributor had resigned and all stamps had been destroyed!

One man, the virtually unknown 29-year-old Patrick Henry

---

[2] Moses Coit Tyler, *Patrick Henry* (Boston: Houghton Mifflin, 1887), p. 73,.
[3] See Henry, *Patrick Henry: Life*, p. 184.

stepped forth to challenge the inevitable and changed the course of our nation's history! The movement to freedom had been launched. Rebellion and the ultimate War of Independence would forever change the world. May 29, 1765, a day—***When Leadership Mattered.***

Bonus Notes

- Having failed as a farmer and twice as a storekeeper, Patrick Henry pursued the law profession. He completed the "reading of the law" in a very short time, and his application was confirmed by George Wythe, Peyton Randolph, and John Randolph. This career paved the way to him becoming a well-known patriot, politician, and ultimately statesman.

- After retiring from political life he made his living by serving as a lawyer. His oratory skills were held in such high esteem, that when he presented the British Debt case before the bar, the Virginia legislature cancelled their session to come hear him. He argued his case for three days, and when he finished his litany against British tyranny there was thunderous applause from the spectators.

- Proof of his exalted reputation was demonstrated in that after his retirement he was offered the positions of ambassador to Spain, Secretary of State, and Chief Justice of the Supreme Court. He was also nominated by the governor to fill the unexpired seat in the United States Senate. And finally, the Republican Party sought him to run for governor, for a sixth term. He refused them all.

- While George Washington is often called the Father of our Nation, Patrick Henry could also be a candidate for that title. He had 17 children, six by his first wife, Sarah, and eleven more by his second wife, Dorothea. These children gave him more than 70 grandchildren

CHAPTER TWO

George Washington

His bold, audacious gamble saved the Revolution!

It was a few days before Christmas, 1776. The American Revolution seemed almost lost. General George Washington's army had not won a battle in five months. The army had dwindled from 20,000 men to about 2,000, and many of those enlistments would end at year's end. They had been routed and driven from New York across New Jersey and were now in Pennsylvania.

The soldiers were exhausted, disheartened, ill-equipped, and poorly fed. In the winter's cold, many were dressed in tattered clothes. Some had no shoes, their feet wrapped in rags. It was a desperate time!

Washington and his men were encamped along the Delaware River on the Pennsylvania or west side of the river. Across the river the British had stationed their dreaded Hessian troops, who were German mercenaries, in four forts along the river, about 10 miles apart from each other.

Washington feared that as soon as the ice on the river was thick enough, there was nothing to stop the enemy from crossing the river to attack them.

The spirit of the army and the fledgling country was one of discouragement and near hopelessness. A bold and dynamic plan to win a victory and save the Revolution was desperately needed.

Washington, himself, burned with the desire to attack. The British had humiliated him in New York. "But more than revenge gnawed at him. Washington knew that the war, and American independence, hung in the balance. Flagging spirits must be revivified."[4]

On December 22, Washington's position was strengthened by the arrival of 600 Continentals brought north by General Horatio Gates, 1,000 Philadelphia militia, a regiment of German settlers from Maryland and Pennsylvania, and the bedraggled 2,000-man remnant of General Charles Lee's troops. Thus for a very short period of time, Washington would have at his disposal "a wretched but usable military force" of some 6,000 men. [5]

He convened a war council with his officers to discuss the desperate situation and to decide which of the garrisons they might attack. There were four possible targets.

There were about 1,500 Hessians in cantonments at both Trenton and Bordentown. There was a smaller force, one battalion of grenadiers, encamped at Burlington. The largest of the enemy forces was at Princeton, about 12 miles from Trenton, with about 2,500 infantry and dragoons. No decision was reached.

Later that evening Washington convened a second war council with fewer officers. This time the decision was made to attack the Hessians at Trenton at dawn on December 26. [6]

The plan was daring and extremely risky, fraught with danger! To succeed it had to be a surprise attack to catch the Hessians off

---

[4] John E. Ferling, *Almost a Miracle: The American Victory in the War of Independence* (New York: Oxford University Press, 2007), p. 172.
[5] Edward G. Lengel, *General George Washington: A Military Life* (New York: Random House, 2005), p. 179.
[6] Ferling, *Almost a Miracle*, 173.

guard.

Washington and his staff had planned the operation in great detail. The plan called for Washington with 2,400 of his most seasoned troops to cross the Delaware River just after dark on December 25, Christmas night, and attack the Hessians at Trenton about an hour before dawn on December 26. They would move the men across on Durham boats, 40- to 60-foot boats used for hauling corn, iron, whiskey, and other cargo down the river to Philadelphia. Eighteen artillery pieces, ammunition, and horses would be carried across on the large Delaware ferries.

The plan also called for several other columns to cross the Delaware at different places and trap the Hessians in Trenton by cutting off all escape roads. They were all to move across the river simultaneously.

Colonel John Cadwalader's 1,200 Philadelphia Associators and 600 New England Continentals would cut the road from Burlington to prevent reinforcements from that fort.

General James Ewing's Pennsylvania militia brigade of about 800 men was to cross the river directly across from Trenton and seize the bridge at Assunpink.[7]

To surprise the Hessians, it was imperative to cross the river at night and make the nine-mile march before dawn. That meant the army needed to finish their crossing of the river and assemble on the New Jersey side by midnight and be ready to march.[8]

As if Washington didn't have enough challenges on this freezing wintry night, as he was leaving his quarters to go to the river he received a letter delivered by a weary major who had ridden all the

---

[7] Ferling, *Almost a Miracle*, p.176.
[8] David Hackett Fischer, *Washington's Crossing* (New York : Oxford University Press, 2004), p. 208.

way from Philadelphia that day.

The letter was from General Horatio Gates, a general whom Washington had asked to take a command in the Trenton operation but who had begged off saying he was ill and needed to go to Philadelphia. Washington learned that in actuality, Gates was bypassing him, going straight to Congress in an attempt to get them to overrule his plan of operations. And maybe, he might be given the nod to replace Washington as the commander.

One can only imagine how receiving this letter from Gates at the exact same time the crossing was beginning made Washington feel. Nevertheless, he did not allow himself to be distracted from the mission by this underhanded maneuvering from a rival.[9]

At about 4 p.m. on Christmas Day drums began to beat, and the regiments began to gather for their normal evening parade or formation. On this day the soldiers had all been told to bring their muskets. Only a few key officers knew anything about the planned operation that was about to get underway. It was a secret mission.

Washington instructed the commanders to have their regiments at their assembly areas near the river before sunset, which was at 4:41 p.m. that day. Unfortunately, this didn't happen. It was well after 6 p.m. when the first regiment got to its crossing site. This story was repeated with all the regiments. Before it even started, the mission was running more than two hours behind schedule.

The painting *Washington Crossing the Delaware*, by Emanuel Leutze, is arguably the best known painting about the Revolutionary War. However, the details of what actually happened that night during the crossing are not widely known.

The real story of the crossing that night and the battle that followed

---

[9]Fischer, *Washington's Crossing*, p. 211.

are awe-inspiring.

Washington and his troops would leave from McConkey's and Johnson's Ferries and cross the Delaware about ten miles above Trenton.

Washington Crossing the Delaware River by Emanuel Leutze

Conditions were terrible. The weather had changed from drizzle at sunset to a driving rain, and by about 11 p.m. "a howling nor'easter hit them with a terrific force." According to the soldier John Greenwood, "it rained, hailed, snowed and froze . . . [and the wind rose so high] it blew a perfect hurricane." [10]

Colonel Henry Knox had been placed in charge of the crossing. He was a tall and large man weighing about 300 lbs. His presence and his deep bass voice was a huge factor in the successful transport that blustery night. Several commanders of the army believed that the crossing would have failed "but for the stentorian lungs of Colonel Knox."[11]

Another key element was Colonel John Glover and his Marblehead

---

[10] Quoted in Fischer, *Washington's Crossing*, p. 212.
[11] Fischer, *Washington's Crossing*, p. 218.

regiment of seamen and fishermen who crewed the boats that night. They propelled the heavy-laden boats with oars or long 18-foot "setting poles." Their work that night was masterful.

The soldiers were crowded into Durham boats that could hold up to forty men. The boats had few if any seats, so during the crossing most all of the men would have been standing. Had they chosen to sit in the bottom of the boat, they would have been sitting in icy water. [12]

Other factors besides the wind and snow added to the difficulty of transporting the troops across the river. The current was swift and huge chunks of ice were swirling in the water, banging into the boats.[13]

According to David Hackett Fischer, "Another problem was the darkness of the night. The storm had obscured the moonlight. Visibility was so poor the boatmen could barely see the opposite shore. Washington thought that the 'greatest fatigue' was 'in breaking a passage through the ice' along the shore."[14]

Finally, the landings were completed. Not a single man was lost during the treacherous crossing. The last boat arrived about 3:00 a.m., about three hours behind schedule. By 4:00 a.m. the troops were assembled across the river and they began the nine-mile march toward Trenton.

The march was fraught with hardship. The roads were winding, steep, muddy, and treacherous to both the men and the horses. "The slanting snow, sleet, and hail drove straight into the faces of men plunging forward in nearly total darkness. At least two men

---

[12] Ron Chernow, *Washington: A Life* (New York: Penguin Press, 2010) p. 273, 217.

[13] John E. Ferling, *The First of Men* (Knoxville: University of Tennessee Press, 1988), p. 184.

[14] Fischer, *Washington's Crossing*, p. 218.

tumbled into roadside snowdrifts and froze to death."[15]

That brutal, freezing trek was made even more difficult by the heavy load the men were carrying. Each man carried a pack, musket and bayonet, sixty rounds of ammunition, three days cooked rations, and a blanket. Some were barefooted or had rags tied about their feet. More than one soldier later recalled seeing bloody footprints in the snow.[16]

After two hours the army had made it to Binghamton, about four miles. It was here that General Sullivan turned right with his column onto the River Road while Washington and Greene's column continued marching down the Princeton Road.

A while later a messenger arrived from Greene and told them they had met no opposition, but their powder was wet and they wouldn't be able to fire their muskets. Washington instructed that they would fight with their bayonets!

At about daybreak Washington's column ran into a small band of about fifty patriots who had been sent by General Adam Stephen to attack a Hessian outpost. Washington had known nothing about this until he met this group on the march to Trenton. He was infuriated! If the Hessians were alerted and ready to fight, the plan would not work and the results might be disastrous.

"You, sir, may have ruined all my plans by having put them on their guard!" Washington said to the captain leading the band of Virginians.[17]

The plan had been to attack the Hessians at Trenton about an hour before daybreak, around 6 a.m. But because of all the delays and

---

[15] Chernow, *Washington: A Life*, p. 274.
[16] Ferling, *Almost a Miracle*, p. 176.
[17] James Thomas Flexner, *George Washington in the American Revolution* (Boston: Little, Brown and Company, 1967), p. 176.

extreme difficulties, it would be 8:00 a.m. when General Washington shouted the order, "Advance and charge!"[18]

General Greene's forces were divided into three columns, with Washington leading the middle column. They attacked the north and west side of Trenton. About three minutes later General Sullivan began his attack on the south side of town. The surprise had worked! The Hessians didn't know they were under attack until the guns opened up. They quickly realized they were being attacked from three directions.

Colonel Johann Rall, the fifty-year-old veteran commander of the Hessians, was still in his nightclothes when his adjutant, Lieutenant Jakob Piel, burst into the room and told him they were under attack. Rall quickly dressed and went outside, mounted his horse and began to try to rally his troops. They were facing withering musket fire from advancing Continental soldiers and fire from Colonel Knox's artillery.

The Hessians rolled out two cannons onto King Street and began to deliver punishing fire on the Americans. The Continentals were able to rush forward and capture the cannons. Rall, however, rallied his men and recaptured the cannons. Then, Captain William Washington, a second cousin to General Washington, and Lieutenant James Monroe, a future president of the United States, led a successful charge to once again seize the cannons. Both men were wounded by musket fire: Washington in both hands and Monroe hit in the chest, severing an artery. A surgeon, Dr. John Riker, a volunteer who had joined the regiment the day before, was able to clamp his wound and save his life.[19]

As the fortunes of battle swung, Rall's men were able to recapture those cannons. They were on the verge of being ready to put them

---

[18] Ferling, *Almost A Miracle*, p. 177.
[19] Fischer, *Washington's Crossing,* p. 247.

into action when Rall was hit once, and then again, by musket balls and fell severely wounded from his horse and was carried into a nearby church.[20]

Without their commander, the fight was quickly over. "The Rall and Lossburg regiments threw up their hands first, and seeing it, the Knyphausen Regiment surrendered too."[21]

The Hessians had lost 22 men killed including Rall with 84 wounded. Nearly 900 men had been captured, but more than 600 had managed to escape.[22]

The battle had lasted less than an hour!

When Washington learned from Major James Wilkinson of the surrender of the last (Hessian) regiment, he beamed and while shaking his hand exclaimed, "this is a glorious day for our country."[23]

Washington's losses were two killed and four slightly wounded.[24] However, several more also died in the next few days as a result of exhaustion and exposure and others still from illnesses related to their ordeal in the forbidding elements.[25]

Washington's victory gave him desperately needed supplies and equipment. "The Americans had taken all the Germans' brass field pieces, six wagons, forty horses, one thousand muskets and

---

[20]Glenn Beck, *Being George Washington: The Indispensable Man, as You've Never Seen Him* (New York: Threshold Editions /Mercury Radio Arts, 2011) p. 32.

[21] Lengel, *General George Washington*, p. 188.

[22] Lengel, *General George Washington*, p. 188.

[23] Chernow, *Washington: A Life,* p. 276.

[24] Lengel, *General George Washington*, p.188. Some accounts, i.e., David Hackett Fischer in *Washington's Crossing*, say that Hamilton was very seriously wounded.

[25] Ferling, *Almost a Miracle*, p. 178.

bayonets, [and] considerable ammunition."[26]

Washington did not know that his other two forces, Cadwalader's 1,800 men and Ewing's Pennsylvania brigade of about 800 men, had not been able to cross the river and get to their objectives because of swift currents and ice flows in the river.[27]

So the battle had been won by just one of the three groups that were supposed to attack or support the attack at Trenton. Had the other two forces succeeded in crossing the river and cutting off the escape routes, Washington might well have captured the entire Hessian garrison of 1,500 men!

This victory was the break Washington needed so desperately at this moment in time. "A happy public gave Washington credit for the victory. . . . Congressmen were lavish in their praise, exalting that the victory 'puts new life' into the Revolution and attributing the turnabout 'entirely to your [Washington's] Wisdom and Conduct.'"[28]

Washington's momentous victory at Trenton re-invigorated the fires of the Revolution. There was a new respect, a new enthusiasm and support for Washington and the Continental Army. In just a few days he would win another victory at Princeton.

News of the victory travelled fast. Within days the news had coursed throughout the thirteen colonies causing people's spirits to rise. A British land buyer named Nicholas Cresswell who was being detained in rural Loudon County, Virginia wrote, "The minds of the people are much altered. A few days ago they had given up the cause for lost. Their late successes have turned the scale and now they are all liberty mad again. Their Recruiting

---

[26] Ferling, *Almost a Miracle*, p. 178.
[27] Ferling, *Almost a Miracle*, p. 176.
[28] Ferling ,*Almost a Miracle*, p. 178.

parties could not get a man (except he bought him from his master) . . . and now the men are coming in by companies." [29]

Though there would be many more challenges and disappointments in the fight for independence, the battle at Trenton was a turning point in the Revolution.

"No single day in history was more decisive for the creation of the United States than Christmas 1776."[30]

General George Washington, with everything at stake, took a very bold gamble - and won. Had he not won this important victory at Trenton, the Revolution would likely have been lost.

Christmas 1776, a time—***When Leadership Mattered.***

Bonus Notes

- During the French and Indian War in 1755, young George Washington served as a colonel in the forces of British General Edward Braddock, Commander in Chief of British forces in America. While their 1,400-man army was advancing through wilderness near French Fort Duquesne, near present-day Pittsburgh, they were ambushed by French, Canadians, and Potawatomi and Ottawa Indians. Washington served as a courier delivering orders for Braddock. Some 900 British soldiers were killed in this devastating attack, including General Braddock. Washington, on horseback, was perilously exposed to the enemy as he rode repeatedly up and down the lines delivering messages from the commander. Miraculously, Washington was not hit even though he had four bullet

---

[29] Quoted in Fischer, *Washington's Crossing*, pp. 259-260.
[30] James McPherson, foreword, Fischer, *Washington's Crossing*, p. ix.

holes through his coat and two horses shot out from under him. Every other officer was shot and either killed or wounded.

- Washington was the only president who was elected unanimously. On February 4, 1789, all 69 members of the Electoral College voted for him as president. Due to terrible road conditions the Congress would be unable to have a quorum to approve him until early April.

- When the war had ended, British King George III learned that Washington had given up command of the army and was planning to return to his farm. The King remarked, "If he does that he will be the greatest man in the world."

- For a glimpse of the impact Washington had, we can consider this: some 241 townships, 26 cities, 15 mountains, and a multitude of institutions, forts, parks, monuments, geological features , etc., are named after him. And, it's not just in America, but around the world.

CHAPTER THREE

Joshua Chamberlain

His leadership convinced nearly 120 deserters to take up arms and return to the fight at one of the most critical moments in the Civil War.

Joshua Lawrence Chamberlain seemed an unlikely hero. He had been a professor of Rhetoric at Bowdoin College in Maine and had no formal military background or training. Yet he now found himself commanding a regiment at arguably the most critical time and place on the most crucial battlefield of the Civil War: July 2, 1863, Gettysburg, Pennsylvania.

General Robert E. Lee had won decisive victories at Fredericksburg and Chancellorsville, and now he had boldly marched deep into Union territory. His army was a looming threat against Baltimore and even the capital, Washington, D.C. If Lee were able to capture the capital or another major city, President Lincoln might be forced to sue for peace and end the war.

Colonel Chamberlain had been given command of the 20th Maine Volunteer Infantry Regiment while on the march to Gettysburg, Pennsylvania. Shortly afterward, General George G. Meade, commander of the Union Army, delivered at bayonet point 120 deserters from a disbanded unit (2nd Maine) to Colonel Chamberlain the day before the momentous battle of Gettysburg.

Chamberlain had the authority to have these men shot as deserters.

Instead, he took time to talk to some of them and hear their story. He found that they had been terribly misled by a recruiting officer and believed their enlistment ended when their regiment was disbanded. It didn't. So they had rebelled against their command and refused to do any military duties.[31]

His off-the-cuff speech to these men has been called by some historians one of the most important speeches of the Civil War. We shall see why a little later in the story.

He spoke to the men as a group just after they arrived.

> I've been ordered to take you men with me, I'm told that if you don't come . . . I can shoot you. Well, you know I won't do that. Maybe somebody else will, but I won't, so that's that. Here's the situation, the whole Reb army is up that road a ways waiting for us, so this is no time for an argument like this, I tell you. We could surely use you fellahs, we're now well below half strength. . . .
>
> This is a different kind of army. If you look back through history you will see men fighting for pay, for women, for some other kind of loot. They fight for land, power, because a king leads them, or just because they like killing. But we are here for something new, this has not happened much, in the history of the world.
>
> We are an army out to set other men free. America should be free ground, all of it, not divided by a line between slave states and free—all the way to the Pacific Ocean. No man has to bow. No man born to royalty. Here we judge you by what you do, not by who your father was. Here you can be something. Here is the place to

---

[31] Joshua Lawrence Chamberlain, *Bayonet! Forward: My Civil War Reminiscences* (Gettysburg, PA: Stan Clark Military Books, 1994), p. 24.

build a home.

But it's not the land, there's always more land. It's the idea that we all have value—you and me. What we are fighting for in the end, we're fighting for each other.

Sorry, I didn't mean to preach. You go ahead and talk for a while. If you choose to join us and want your muskets back you can have them—nothing more will be said by anyone anywhere. If you choose not to join us, well then you can come along under guard and when this is all over I will do what I can to ensure you get a fair trial, but for now we're moving out.

Gentlemen, I think if we lose this fight we lose the war, so if you choose to join us, I will be personally very grateful.[32]

After Chamberlain's talk with the men, 114 of the 120 immediately decided to take their muskets back, and an additional 4 within several days. These man would play a crucial part in the coming battle.

Chamberlain's 20th Maine regiment reached the heights southeast of Gettysburg at about 7:00 a.m. on July 2 with only an hour or two of sleep before marching. After moving to the left several times during the day, at about 4 p.m. a sharp cannonade

Brigadier General Joshua Chamberlain

was the signal for the whole division to move rapidly to the left. They were at the edge of some woods, receiving heavy musket fire

---

[32] Chamberlain, qtd. in Phil Dourado, "The Speech That Changed The Course of the US Civil War," *theleadershiphub*, April 2, 2012.

and were about to move forward when they received orders from Colonel Strong Vincent, commander of the brigade, to move to the left at a double-quick, in order to gain a rugged mountain spur called Little Round Top. Vincent told Chamberlain that his unit would be the extreme left of their general line and to expect a desperate attack in order for the enemy to turn or flank that position. His final words to him were "hold this ground at all hazards"; Vincent would be killed later that day.[33]

Once the 20th Maine occupied Little Round Top the Confederates attacked on the left flank, advancing to within a dozen yards before the withering fire from the Yanks compelled them to break off the attack. They then renewed their attack along the whole front and for an hour the fighting was severe. In some places squads of enemy soldiers broke through the line. The fighting was hand to hand. The edge of the battle ebbed and flowed. Chamberlain's men would be pushed back from their position and then recover it. His men were able to gather ammunition from the cartridge boxes of dead soldiers—both friend and foe.

Chamberlain feared that his line would be unable to stop another all-out assault by the enemy. Half of his left wing was down and a full one third of the regiment lay behind the lines either dead or wounded.

At this time Chamberlain heard the roar of muskets to his rear and he feared the enemy might have surrounded Little Round Top. With their ammunition almost gone, his men were down to their last shots. It was a time of desperation.

He believed that it was imperative that he attack the enemy before they attacked him again. He gave the word, "Bayonet." The word ran like wildfire through the unit, rapidly passing from man to

---

[33] Chamberlain, *Bayonet! Forward*, p. 204.

man. They rose in a shout and sprang toward the enemy now only about thirty yards away.

"The effect was surprising; many of the enemy's first line threw down their arms and surrendered. . . . Holding fast by our right, and swinging forward our left, we made an extended 'right wheel,' before the enemy's second line broke and fell back, fighting from tree to tree, many being captured, until we had swept the valley and cleared the front of nearly our entire brigade."[34]

When the fighting on little Round Top ended, some 400 rebel prisoners had been taken and 150 of the enemy were dead or wounded.

The 20th Maine had just barely been able to hold Little Round Top against vicious repeated attacks. Had Chamberlain not taken the time to listen and talk to those deserters, convincing them to take up their muskets that day and be in the line at that critical place and time, they could not have stopped the desperate Confederate onslaught that day.

If the Confederates had been successful in seizing Little Round Top, the whole Union line would have faced withering, enfilading fire from that mount and would have had to give up the field. This would have given Lee a tremendous victory!

Instead of suffering a disastrous defeat on July 3 with the failure of Pickett's Charge and leaving Gettysburg defeated, depleted, and demoralized, Lee would have been able to leave victorious. His army could then directly threaten Washington, D.C. The whole tide of the war might well have turned in the favor of the South.

Chamberlain would go on to have many more successes in the Civil War, including winning the Medal of Honor, receiving the

---

[34] Chamberlain, *Bayonet! Forward*, p. 206.

only battlefield promotion given by General Ulysses Grant, and having the high honor of being selected to receive the surrender of Confederate forces at Appomattox. After the war he would also serve as governor of Maine for four terms and later serve as president of Bowdoin College, his alma mater, for twelve years.

But of all the successes he would ever have, none was more important than holding that key ground atop Little Round Top, in that desperate fight that was so pivotal to the battle of Gettysburg and consequently important to the outcome of our nation's Civil War.

On July 2, 1863, Colonel Joshua Chamberlain and the 20th Maine held Little Round Top on a day—***When Leadership Mattered.***

Bonus Notes

- He fought in more than 20 battles. He was wounded six times and had six horses shot from under him during the Civil War.

- His most serious wound occurred at the second battle of Petersburg. He was shot through the hips, and the bullet cut his bladder and urethra. He thought the wound was fatal and kept standing, leaning on his sword as long as possible to rally his soldiers in the battle. Eventually he collapsed and was carried to the field hospital where again his bravery and devotion was apparent as he insisted that the doctors tend to the other wounded before him. They disobeyed him and were able to save his life.

- Chamberlain was also gravely ill twice during the war.

- Because of his perseverance and doggedness in overcoming wounds and illness, his comrades and soldiers gave him the nickname the "Lion of the Union."

CHAPTER FOUR

Theodore Roosevelt

His bold, dynamic leadership helped usher in "The American Century."

Theodore (Teddy) Roosevelt is known as one of the boldest, most courageous and audacious men in American history. His indomitable spirit, sometimes compared to a bull-in-a-china shop, and his can-do attitude helped lead America out of isolationism and into a prominent place as a world leader!

Roosevelt was an intriguing leader and one of the most fun, dynamic, irrepressible characters to ever mount our national stage.

He was the quintessential adventurer, a cowboy, explorer, soldier, hunter, and rancher, yet he was also a respected scholar, author, historian, botanist, environmentalist, and politician.

Born into affluence in the heart of New York City, as a child "Teddy" was an unlikely candidate to become a symbol for an adventure-seeking, strong man of action. He suffered from debilitating asthma. He often had asthma attacks at night, and his father would take him for fast carriage rides in the night air, hoping to help him breathe more easily.

When he was told by a doctor that he needed to expand his lung capacity, he began to strenuously work out to build his body and improve his health. He discovered that as he physically exerted himself, he not only got stronger, his asthma improved, and it bolstered his spirits. After being roughed up by a couple of boys on a camping trip when he was about 12 years old, he took boxing lessons from an ex-prize fighter so he could learn to defend himself. Three years later, he won a trophy for being the best Lightweight boxer in his local gym. Roosevelt was not one to let adversity get the best of him. When faced with challenges, he always doubled down to fight and change the situation.

On February 12, 1884, while he was away in Albany serving in the New York General Assembly, his wife Alice gave birth to a daughter, Alice Lee. The first telegram he received the next day said the baby was ok, but that his wife was "only fairly well." However, a second telegram came a few hours later and instructed him to come home as quickly as possible because his wife had taken a turn for the worse.

He took the train and arrived home near midnight to find both his wife and his mother gravely ill. His sweet wife was so sick she could barely recognize him. He stayed with her for a couple of hours until he was summoned to go to his mother if he wanted to see her alive.

At 3:00 a.m. his beloved mother died. He returned to his wife's side and watched helplessly as she slowly slipped away. She was only 22 years old when she passed away at 2 p.m. Roosevelt was in a total state of shock and bewilderment. He was devastated.

Unexpectedly, on the same day, in the same house, he had lost the two women most precious to him in his life. In his journal that day he would draw a large black X at the top of the page and under it write, "The light has gone out of my life."[35] There was a double funeral for his wife and mother. Three days later he was back at the General Assembly, pouring himself into his work. He refused to

---

[35] Roger L. Di Silvestro, *Theodore Roosevelt in the Badlands: A Young Politician's Quest for Recovery in the American West* (New York: Walker and Company, 2011), p. 61.

be consoled, wanted no one's sympathy, and refused to talk about the deaths of his wife and mother. He just put his total focus and effort into his work.

Roosevelt Goes to the Badlands

In June Roosevelt traveled to the Badlands of North Dakota. Nothing in Roosevelt's life would have as profound an effect on him as his time in the Dakota Badlands.

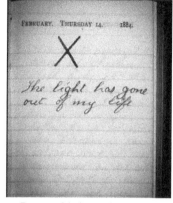

Roosevelt's journal entry on the day his mother and his wife died.

He would spend much of the next three years in the Dakota Badlands ranching, hunting, exploring, and writing, while occasionally returning east to check on family, business, and politics. This time of adventure, hardship, and challenge in the Badlands formed him into the man who would not only lead the nation as president but become a national icon symbolizing physical and mental toughness and an indomitable spirit.

Believing that free grazing and ranching in the Badlands could be very financially lucrative, he bought two ranches, the Maltese Cross Ranch and the Elkhorn Ranch near present-day Medora, North Dakota.

He poured himself into ranching, just like anything else he attempted. While he wasn't particularly talented in roping and branding, he always strived to do his fair share, to pull his own weight.

Roosevelt also made time for big game hunting, which he enjoyed tremendously. He was an avid hunter, not always the best shot, but always the most dogged and determined. He was able to bag every major game animal on the plains and in the mountains. Much of the meat from the hunted animals went to help feed his cowhands. He didn't believe in culling his own herd of cattle to feed his ranch hands but instead preferred to feed them as much as possible with wild game.

During these years he became much stronger and physically tougher. He endured much privation and danger while hunting and ranching. He also had opportunities to chase down robbers, fight in a saloon, have head-to-head confrontations with fellow ranchers, and become the founder and leader of the Little Missouri River Stockmen's Association.

Roosevelt also had to overcome the initial impression he made on the tough westerners. He had the appearance of an "Eastern dude" or a "dandy." He carried ivory-handled six shooters engraved with scrollwork and plated in silver and gold, and he wore silver spurs, and alligator boots. No one else carried a fancy Bowie hunting knife made at Tiffany's in New York City. His rifle was engraved with silver and gold, also done at Tiffany's. His clothes were tailored buckskins. He had thick glasses and a somewhat high and excitable voice. This all went together to make quite an initial impression on folks.

But he also had a very energetic personality and a thoroughly positive or "bully" attitude as he called it. This captivating attitude drew people to his side. So in spite of his appearance and voice, he was usually able to win folks over after they had been around him for just a short while.

One example of this was Jack Willis, a hunting guide from Thompson Falls, Montana, who made this observation: "There was something of the savor of the West in his manner and his frankness, and so long as I could keep my eyes away from his foolish pants, I cottoned to the things he said and the way he said them. In about an hour he had made me forget his knickers and had won me over as far as I would ever go for any man."[36]

In 1886 Roosevelt ran for mayor in New York City. He lost. In that same year he also married an old childhood sweetheart, Edith Kermit Carow.

Police Commissioner

In 1895 after about six years of shaking things up with his reforms while serving as the Commissioner of the U.S. Civil Service, he was offered the job as Commissioner of the New York City Police. He jumped at the chance to serve in this capacity.

He immediately began implementing controversial new reforms in the department. He fired the Police Chief within a few weeks. He hired a woman to be his secretary (unheard in those days), hired minorities as officers, and stopped the practice of paying for promotions. He made the officers attend pistol practice and started requiring physical exams. He also had a telephone system installed.

He gained notoriety as he began conducting undercover midnight patrols to check up on the officers. He would wear a dark cape and have his hat pulled down low. Soon the word was out around the city. People took notice. He was changing things![37]

Assistant Secretary of the Navy

When William McKinley was elected president, Roosevelt quickly began lobbying the administration for a position.

In April 1897 he was appointed the Assistant Secretary of the Navy. It did not take him long to be noticed. Many evenings when

---

[36] Quoted in Di Silvestro, *Theodore Roosevelt in the Badlands*, p. 222.
[37] Betsy Harvey Kraft, *Theodore Roosevelt: Champion of the American Spirit* (New York: Clarion Books, 2003), pp. 41-46.

he dined at Washington's Metropolitan Club, he would be surrounded by many of the Capital's elite, elected officials, and military officers. He wasted no opportunity to loudly and energetically tell them his views on how the United States needed to become stronger and be a player on the world stage. He was particularly concerned about Spain and their possession of the Philippines and their entrenchment in Cuba. He strongly believed that they had no business in the Western Hemisphere. He was a huge advocate of the Monroe Doctrine that prohibited European involvement in the Westerner Hemisphere.

During his tenure as the Assistant Secretary of the Navy, he made numerous trips around the country and gave many speeches to military and civic organizations. He also befriended many major newspaper editors and tried to enlist them and their newspapers to his way of thinking about a greater role for the nation in world affairs. These friendly relations with reporters and editors would pay off handsomely for him in the coming months and years.

Since the Secretary of the Navy, John Long, had this very exuberant and energetic Assistant Secretary, he felt free to leave Washington often and left much of the running of the Navy to Roosevelt. He would sometimes take leaves for weeks at a time. This gave Roosevelt much latitude in running the Navy.

Meanwhile rebels in Cuba had risen up against Spanish rule. The Spanish treated the Cuban rebels and their families very harshly. Public opinion in America resided with the rebels. When riots broke out in Cuba, President McKinley felt that American citizens might need protection, so he sent the mighty American battleship, the U. S. S. Maine, to Havana Harbor.

On the night of February 15, 1898, a huge explosion rocked the Maine killing more than 250 American sailors and officers. Whether the cause of the explosion was accidental or a deliberate act of war was unknown, but major newspaper publishers like William Randolph Hearst and Joseph Pulitzer immediately blamed Spain for the explosion, thus fanning the flames for war. After all, a war would certainly help boost newspaper sales.

McKinley called for calm and ordered an investigation into the explosion. Meanwhile, Navy Secretary Long left the office one afternoon for a doctor's appointment leaving Roosevelt in charge. This was the opening Roosevelt wanted. He sprang into action and ordered the commander of the Pacific Fleet to prepare the fleet, keep it full of coal, and be prepared to keep Spanish ships away from Cuba and to do battle in the Philippines.

Roosevelt didn't really have the authority to ready the fleet and put them on alert, but he did . . . and the order stood.

Soon President McKinley yielded to the pressure from the hawks to fight the Spanish. War was declared on Spain by Congress on April 25, 1898. [38]

Within two weeks of war being declared, Roosevelt resigned as Assistant Secretary of the Navy. He wanted to go fight. He yearned to be in the middle of the action.

President McKinley put out a call for 125,000 volunteer soldiers to augment the small standing army of just 28,000 men. Roosevelt decided he wanted to help raise a volunteer unit, the First U.S. Volunteer Cavalry Regiment. He would be a lieutenant colonel, the second in command, while his friend, the very experienced Indian fighter and Medal of Honor winner, Leonard Wood, was named as the colonel and given command of the unit.

The unit would be known as the Rough Riders since it would be a cavalry unit composed of men such as cowboys who were expert

---

[38] Kraft, *Theodore Roosevelt*, pp. 47-54.

riders and handy with guns. Before long it would be known as Roosevelt's Rough Riders.

This regiment would become probably the most colorful, most eclectic unit ever raised in the United States Army. It not only attracted cowboys but also Native Americans, miners, lawmen, several small town mayors, five ministers, criminals, and even some Ivy League boys from Harvard, Yale, and Columbia, several of whom were top athletes. Before it was all over, some 23,000 men had volunteered for the 1,000 positions in Roosevelt's Rough Rider regiment.

The unit assembled and trained in San Antonio, Texas. When their training was completed, the unit was ordered to move by train to Tampa, Florida, where they would board a ship to Cuba.

Once they arrived in Tampa, they learned they would be unable to ship their mounts to Cuba as there was simply not enough room on the ship. Only the regimental officers' horses could be sent. This was a huge blow to a unit that had trained as a horse-mounted cavalry unit, not as dismounted infantrymen.

Another added indignity was soon realized: not all the men of the unit would be allowed to deploy to Cuba. There was simply not enough room on the ship. Only 560 off the nearly 1,000 men of the regiment would be able to board the ship.[39]

Getting the regiment the final ten miles from their bivouac site to the port of Tampa proved a challenge. General William Shafter, commander of all land forces in Cuba, had supposedly arranged for trains and shipment to the port, but the trains did not materialize.

Finally, Lieutenant Colonel Roosevelt was able to stop a slow

---

[39] Peggy Samuels and Harold Samuels, *Teddy Roosevelt at San Juan: The Making of a President* (College Station: Texas A & M University Press, 1997), p. 76.

moving cargo train and, by hook or by crook—bribery, force, persuasion? no one knows for sure—was able to get his men and equipment loaded onto the train's dusty coal cars and make the final journey to the Port Tampa yard.

At the port all was confusion. The regimental commander, Colonel Wood, was told that the regiment would be loaded on to the *Yucatan*, a freighter. The problem was the ship was also scheduled to carry three other regiments that would have totaled four times the amount of troops the ship could carry.

Wood quickly got a launch to carry him to the *Yucatan* while Roosevelt went back to the troops and marched them at quick time to the pier where they loaded the ship. Roosevelt put a guard at the gangplank to prevent other units from attempting to board the vessel.

When another regiment that had been slotted to be aboard the *Yucata*n arrived, an officer called out and said, "That's our ship." Roosevelt ended the discussion quickly by remarking, "We seem to have it." The other unit eventually learned the lesson that the Rough Riders had demonstrated and went to seize their own ship for transport.[40]

The invasion of Cuba was delayed for about a week causing the soldiers to suffer in extremely cramped conditions aboard the ship loaded to double its capacity. Finally, on June 14 the flotilla of 53 ships that included 35 transports, 14 warships, and 4 auxiliary ships, set sail on the three-day voyage to Cuba.

Cuba at Last

When the convoy of ships arrived at Cuba, the men of the regiment were offloaded at Daiquiri where there was no substantial dock—

---

[40] Samuels and Samuels, *Teddy Roosevelt at San Juan*, p. 80.

only a rickety pier. Many men chose to swim ashore, resulting in two men drowning. Also, one of Roosevelt's horses drowned in the surf.

Much of the regiment's supplies, including food, blankets, and ammunition, were lost during the landing. Not a great beginning.

The next morning the unit began its seven-mile march in oppressive heat to a village where they turned north and headed toward a mountain pass. More than 2,000 Spanish soldiers guarded the pass at Las Guasimas.

As they approached Las Guasimas bullets from the Spanish began to fly. Americans were killed and wounded as they worked their way up toward the enemy. The advantage the Americans had over the Spanish was their very accurate rifle fire. Soon the Spanish pulled out and left the mountain.

General Shafter ordered the regiment to withdraw and do reconnoitering. They remained in the jungle for several days, fighting mosquitos and other insects and land crabs, as well as the sweltering heat.

The Battle of San Juan Hill

Finally the word came to move forward to San Juan Heights. This was a series of hills overlooking Santiago and its harbor.

At 8:00 a.m. on the morning of July 1, 1898, the order was given for the American cannon crews to commence firing on the Spanish atop San Juan Hill. For about 15 minutes or so there was no return fire. Then the Spanish artillery started returning fire. One Rough Rider was killed and three fell wounded. Roosevelt would suffer his first of three wounds that day. The first wound was caused by a piece of shrapnel hitting his left wrist. While it didn't break the skin, it did cause a small knot or bump. Roosevelt proudly wrapped his bandana around his swollen wrist and said to those around him, "Well, that's the first one. They'll have to do better next time."[41]

Roosevelt led his men to a covered area under withering fire. They crossed a stream running red with blood and took cover on the other side.

Under effective fire from enemy Mausers from both front and rear, the Rough Riders kept sustaining casualties without being able to advance or even return fire. This was maddening to Roosevelt. He felt that if his regiment was not used in an attack soon, they would be so diminished by casualties and the oppressive heat that they might become totally ineffective.

Roosevelt kept waiting for orders to advance. None came. At about 11:30 a.m., after receiving punishing fire from the Spanish for an hour, Roosevelt formed his regiment into a column of troops and began to advance them toward Kettle Hill. His unit, the 1st Volunteer Regiment, had actually been placed in a reserve or rear position and was behind the 9th and 10th Cavalry Regiments when they started to move.

Finally an order came to Roosevelt to support the 10th Regiment from behind when they conducted their assault. However, by this time Roosevelt had already been advancing his regiment for 15 minutes or so. He just kept pushing his men forward. While his men advanced in rushes, maybe six feet at a time, he sat mounted atop on his horse, the most exposed man in the regiment.

One witness, a news reporter said, "No one who saw Roosevelt take that ride expected that he would finish it alive."[42] Later he

---

[41] Samuels and Samuels, *Teddy Roosevelt at San Juan*, p. 218.

[42] Quoted in Stephanie Sammartino McPherson, *Theodore Roosevelt* (Minneapolis, MN: Lerner Publications, 2005), p. 54.

was forced to dismount because of a fence and continued up the hill on foot.

While there is some debate about who actually gave the initial order for the regiments to charge, there is no debate that Roosevelt soon took the lead riding ahead of all his dismounted cavalry. At some point a bullet knocked the glasses off his head. He had a replacement pair at the ready.

Soon the outnumbered Spaniards on Kettle Hill were driven off and retreated toward San Juan Heights. While the Rough Riders were on top of the knoll Roosevelt was hit again by an enemy bullet. This time he was nicked in the elbow and bled freely.

The Regiment atop Kettle Hill was receiving lethal fire from San Juan Hill, which was being attacked by other units. Roosevelt held a brief meeting with his officers and told them they were going to attack San Juan Hill and he would lead the charge.

When Roosevelt gave his unit the command to charge and attack San Juan Hill, he initially was followed by only 5 men out of the 500 or so in the unit. When he noticed the rest had not followed, he quickly ran back to the top of the knoll and chastised the men for not following him. They told him that they had not heard his command to charge. When he gave the order again, they followed.

As they advanced by a pond on the way up the slopes of the hill, Roosevelt was struck on the back of his left hand by a spent bullet. This was his third minor wound of the day.

By the time he and his men reached the top of San Juan Hill, other units, the 6th and 3rd Cavalry, had already gotten there. However, Roosevelt had one last chance for glory. Two Spaniards jumped up from the trenches and fired at Roosevelt and his accomplice. . . . they missed. As they turned to flee, Roosevelt pulled out a pistol that had been recovered from the Maine and fired at both of the men, killing one. His accomplice quickly dispatched the other

Teddy Roosevelt and the Rough Riders at San Juan Hill

man.

The war in Cuba only lasted eleven days. It ended a few days after the battle of San Juan Hill when the American navy destroyed the Spanish fleet outside of Santiago harbor.

Teddy Roosevelt came home a national hero. "Full page photo engravings of him, dressed in his khaki uniform, campaign hat, and navy blue and white polka dot neckerchief appeared on the covers and inside such popular weekly journals as *Harper's* and *Leslie's.*

Roosevelt would wear the image of a Rough Rider for the rest of his life."[43]

From Governor to President

Within a few weeks after returning home from Cuba he was nominated for governor of New York. He was elected that fall to the two-year term as governor.

Soon the political boss in New York, Senator Thomas Platt, who was used to running all things political in the state, found out he could not run Roosevelt. He began looking for a way to get rid of him. In 1900 President William McKinley needed a running mate since his vice president, Garret A. Hobart, had recently died. So, Platt began a campaign to have Roosevelt nominated to run for Vice President. This move was perfect for Platt. It would make Roosevelt's supporters happy and get him out of his hair in New York.[44]

At the Republican Convention that summer Roosevelt was almost unanimously selected as the nominee for Vice President. The vote was 925 to 1. The one "no" vote against him was his own.

In November, 1900, the ticket of McKinley and Roosevelt handily defeated their opponents led by William Jennings Bryan. Now at the age of 42, the youngest vice president in history, he was only a heartbeat away from being the president of the United States.

When McKinley was assassinated less than one year later, Theodore Roosevelt became the 26th president of the United States of America. He would finish McKinley's term and then handily win reelection for another term. He served as president from 1901

---

[43] James G. Barber, *Theodore Roosevelt: Icon of the American Century* (Seattle: University of Washington Press, 1998), p. 38.
[44] Sean McCollum, Theodore Roosevelt: America's 26th President (N. p.: Children's Press, 2004), pp. 40-43.

until 1909.

While serving as president he helped America change from its isolationism mindset and become a world power. He projected American power to the world. In 1907 he sent his "Great White Fleet," a force of 16 U. S. Navy warships on an around-the-world mission to show American military strength and to help build national pride. The warships sailed some 46,000 miles, circumnavigating the globe in 14 months. The flotilla was the first naval group in the world to sail completely around the world.

Roosevelt demonstrated his great political and public relations savvy by sending a reporter along with the fleet so that their amazing voyage could be reported to America and the rest of the world.

As president he built up the U. S. Navy from being the 5th largest to 2nd largest navy in the world, second only to that of Great Britain. He wanted to be able to deploy them quickly to areas where American power needed to be demonstrated. Early on he saw the need for a canal to cut through Central America, allowing access to ships to cross from the Atlantic to the Pacific (or vice versa) without having to sail all the way down to the southern tip of South America. Thus, it was at his direction that the Panama Canal was constructed. This enabled America to project significant naval power around the world. America would control this gateway for the entire twentieth century.

A Great Leader in Conservation

Roosevelt was also very interested in preserving the beauty and tranquility of our nation's bountiful wilderness areas, as well as protecting the wildlife. While he was president more than 230 million acres were designated as public lands. The list included 5 new national parks, 18 national monuments, 4 national game preserves, 51 federal bird reservations, 150 national forests, and 24 reclamation projects. It was a record unequaled by any other president.[45]

There are many reasons that the likeness of Teddy Roosevelt is included on Mount Rushmore. His strong, hardy, self-reliant, cowboy, adventuresome, Rough-Rider mentality left an indelible imprint on America with his infectious enthusiasm and can-do spirit!

In those early days of the twentieth century when America was in a time of great transition, Theodore Roosevelt exhibited bold, dynamic leadership that helped usher in "the American Century" when the U.S became a world leader in military and economic power. His indomitable spirit was infused into the very fabric of America.

Teddy Roosevelt helped establish our national identity. This bold and courageous statesman helped make America a prominent world leader during the twentieth century, fighting tyranny and despotism, helping establish democracies, and bringing humanitarian aid to those in need around the globe—even to our enemies.

Teddy Roosevelt was there in the early 1900s—***When Leadership Mattered***.

---

[45] Kraft, Champion of the American Spirit, p. 121.

"THE MAN IN THE ARENA," From his 1910 Speech

> It is not the critic who counts; not the man who points out how the strong man stumbles, or where the doer of deeds could have done them better. The credit belongs to the man who is actually in the arena, whose face is marred by dust and sweat and blood; who strives valiantly; who errs, who comes short again and again, because there is no effort without error and shortcoming; but who does actually strive to do the deeds; who knows great enthusiasms, the great devotions; who spends himself in a worthy cause; who at the best knows in the end the triumph of high achievement, and who at the worst, if he fails, at least fails while daring greatly, so that his place shall never be with those cold and timid souls who neither know victory nor defeat.[46]

The passage above is probably one of Teddy Roosevelt's best known quotes. It epitomizes him! He was definitely a man who was always "in the arena . . .whose face is marred by dust and sweat and blood."

Bonus Notes

- While running for a third term as a presidential candidate, he was shot in the chest by a would-be assassin. He refused medical care, went into the meeting room, and delivered a 1 ½ hour speech (bloody shirt and all) before he would allow himself to be carried to a hospital.

- He won the Nobel Peace Prize for his work in helping

---

[46] Theodore Roosevelt, excerpt from his speech, "Citizenship in a Republic: The Man in the Arena," delivered at the Sorbonne, Paris, France, April 23, 1910.

Russia and Japan come to agreement after their war. He was the first American to win it.

- He was known as fastest hand-shaker in history. He averaged 50 grips per minute.

- As young boys, he and his cousin started the Roosevelt Museum of Natural History in a bedroom. He developed a good, rudimentary knowledge of taxidermy.

- He once spent three weeks hunting alone on the prairie.

- His army uniform in Spanish American War was made for him in New York City by Brooks Brothers.

- He published 35 books in his lifetime.

- He was the first president to fly in an airplane (1910), go down in a submarine, own a car, and have a telephone in his home.

- While serving as president, he always carried a gun.

- He and his brother Elliott watched Abraham Lincoln's funeral procession from the 2nd floor window of his grandfather's house in New York City. Thirty-six years later he would be president of the United States.

- During his second inauguration he wore a ring on his right hand with strands of Abraham Lincoln's hair in it.

- He wrote more than 150,000 letters, averaging about 10 per day for 40 years.

- It was said he laughed 100 times a day with the same energy as he talked.

- He almost died from a severe leg injury while on an expedition of an uncharted tributary of the Amazon River.

- He was a voracious reader and always carried or had books immediately available, whether hunting, exploring, or in the White House. He kept a variety of books on various subjects ranging from physics to poetry, navy to naturalist, botany to biographies. He was almost never without books.

- He participated in President Ulysses S. Grant's funeral as a captain in the National Guard.

- He was immensely popular both in the United States and abroad. Once when he traveled abroad after his presidency—a hunting trip and other travel—upon his return he was met by 100, 000 people upon his return to New York City.

- Roosevelt was awarded the Congressional Medal of Honor posthumously 100 years after his death for his action at San Juan, Cuba. The medal was awarded by President William ("Bill") J. Clinton to Roosevelt's great grandson, Tweed Roosevelt, in the Roosevelt Room of the White House.[47]

- He was the first U.S. president to travel to another country while in office.

---

[47] Kraft, *Theodore Roosevelt*, p. 65.

CHAPTER FIVE

Winston Churchill

Winston Churchill "mobilized the English language and sent it into battle." Edward Murrow (1954)

Words have power! And, when used effectively by a leader, they can mobilize a nation to victory.

During the dark, early days of World War II when Adolph Hitler's army was smashing its way through Europe subduing one nation after another, one strong voice emerged to challenge him. That voice was Winston Churchill, the newly appointed prime minister of Great Britain.

On May 10, 1940, Churchill became prime minister. He was "already 65 and, as he put it, ' qualified to draw the Old Age Pension,'"[48] yet his bold, courageous words stirred the souls and stiffened the resolve of not only his native Englishmen, but the rest of the world as well.

Many people across Europe believed it was impossible to defeat Hitler. At his trial years later, a leading French collaborator, Pierre Laval, tried to explain his excuse for not fighting Hitler by asking who in their right mind would have believed in anything but a German victory. There was at least one person who didn't believe it: Winston Churchill.

---

[48] Winston S. Churchill, qtd, in Winston Churchill, *Never Give In! The Best of Winston Churchill's Speeches* (New York: Hyperion, 2003), p. xxi.

While other leaders in Britain were ready to give up or talk to Hitler about "terms," Churchill stood firm! He alone was the backbone of Britain and European resistance to what seemed like an indomitable force.

Appeasement

For the seven years since Hitler had seized power in Germany in 1933, the leaders of Europe had done little to challenge him, but sought to appease him at every turn.

They could have stopped him in March of 1935 when Hitler, in direct violation of the Treaty of Versailles (the peace treaty signed at the end of World War I), ordered the rebuilding of the German military.

In response to the protests of Great Britain and France, Hitler offered vague promises of peace that their governments gratefully accepted. They had no stomach for another war, and his promises gave cover to their cowardice. Meanwhile, Hitler continued building Germany's military strength at breakneck speed.

They could have stopped him a year later when Hitler again tested the resolve of the two nations by marching German troops into the demilitarized Rhineland—another substantial violation of the Treaty of Versailles.

The contingent of troops was a small, token force of only three battalions, less than 2,000 troops. The German commander was under orders to withdraw immediately if there was any military response from France. There was none!

Even though France had about 350,000 troops, they and their ally, Britain, took no action. They did nothing again but protest. Hitler was buoyed by his unchallenged success.

One of Hitler's goals was to consolidate all German-speaking people in Europe under German control. When the Austrian president, Wilhelm Miklas, refused at Hitler's urging to appoint a pro-Nazi chancellor, German foreign minister Hermann Goering took actions to create a "crisis." He had a member of the Austrian government (who was in reality a German agent) issue a plea for German assistance. Hitler used this fake "crisis" as an excuse to invade.

On March 12, 1938, German troops marched into tiny Austria unopposed, and Hitler announced the *Anschluss* (union) between Austria and Germany. He brokered a plebiscite a month later for the "official" vote of the Austrians on the matter of *Anschluss*.

Whether the vote was true or rigged, it is certain Austrians felt the intimidation of the German army inside their borders. When the votes were tallied, 99.7% of the people had voted "yes" for the union. Austria had been annexed and was now part of greater Germany.

The British responded once again with a formal protest which was contemptuously rejected by Adolph Hitler. Again, no action was taken.

The final coup de grace of appeasement was the Munich Agreement. The leaders of Germany, Britain, France, and Italy met for a conference in Munich, Germany, in late September, 1938. At this conference Germany demanded that the Sudeten districts of Czechoslovakia that bordered Germany and contained three million ethnic Germans be given to Germany.

The Czechs refused to give in to Hitler's demand and asked France to honor their pledge to defend them. However, the weak-kneed leaders of France and Britain, Edouard Daladier and Neville Chamberlain, again sought to appease Hitler and allowed him to seize the Sudeten districts. They returned home with a promise from Hitler that there would be no further territorial claims in Europe. British Prime Minister Neville Chamberlain returned to London and proudly proclaimed we have achieved "peace with honor."

The Munich agreement gave Hitler the Sudetenland at first, but ultimately all of Czechoslovakia.

It is worth noting that had France chosen to fight at this time, they had 100 army divisions and the Czechs had 35 well-equipped divisions. But once again, weak leaders tried appeasing Hitler hoping to avoid another war. Appeasement did not work.

In the early days Britain and France could have easily stopped Hitler and the Nazis in their tracks had they displayed any resolve or courage at all.

Today, as the influence and power of radical Islam is rapidly expanding, there are valuable lessons the West can learn by studying Britain and France's weak, ineffective responses to Hitler's aggressive actions from 1935-1939.

One year later, Hitler's military forces, now formidable, were ready for war! On September 1, 1939, one and one half million German soldiers poured across the border of Poland. The Poles valiantly fought back against this massive "*blitzkrieg*" lightning attack but were quickly overwhelmed. The Polish Air Force was destroyed in only 48 hours. By the end of two weeks the Polish government had fled to Romania.

The British, finally showing some courage, demanded a German withdrawal. It became obvious rather quickly that wasn't going to happen, so they, along with France, Australia, and New Zealand, declared war on Germany on September 3. A week later Canada also declared war on Germany and the Battle of the Atlantic began.

By mid-September thousands of British Expeditionary Forces had been sent to the Franco-Belgian border to aid in the defense of France. Then for the next eight months, the "Phoney War" took place on the Western front. The two warring sides took almost no offensive action but mostly sat in entrenchments and stared at each other.

Seven months later on April 9, 1940, the German army went on the offensive again as the Nazis invaded Denmark and Norway.

On May 10, 1940, the Nazis invaded France, Belgium, The Netherlands, and Luxembourg. With this *blitzkrieg* attack on their neighbors and allies, Britain could no longer look the other way. Real, full-blown war was at their doorsteps!

On that same day, Winston Churchill was appointed Prime Minister of Britain by King George VI. Things were about to change.

On May 13 Churchill spoke to the House of Commons, hoping to gain affirmation for his new administration. In his first speech to the House that day Churchill at once brought clarity, direction and resolve to his nation. In his speech he said,

> We have before us an ordeal of the most grievous kind. We have before us many, many long months of struggle and of suffering. You ask, what is our policy? I can say: It is to wage war, by sea, land and air, with all our might and with all the strength that God can give us; to wage war against a monstrous tyranny never surpassed in the dark lamentable catalog of human crime. That is our policy. You ask, what is our aim? I can answer in one word; it is victory, victory at all costs, victory in spite of all terror, victory no matter how long and hard the road may be; for without victory there is no survival. Let that

be realized; no survival for the British Empire, no survival for all that the British Empire has stood for, no survival for the urge and impulse of the ages, that mankind will move forwards toward its goal. But I take up my task with buoyancy and hope. I feel sure that our cause will not be suffered to fail among men. At this time I feel entitled to claim the aid of all, and I say, "Come then, let us go forward together with our united strength."[49]

Finally, Great Britain had a leader! This speech was carried on the radio throughout Britain, Europe, the United States, and all over the world. The effect was stirring and inspiring!

His words were clear, direct, and unambiguous. He intended to wage war on sea, land, and air. And, he intended to have Victory!

However, Churchill was still in a precarious political situation in his own government. He still did not have the backing of the War Cabinet and of major opposition party leaders that he desperately needed.

In the following two weeks, Holland surrendered on May 15. On May 26 the perilous evacuation of some 338,000 British and French troops at Dunkirk began, Belgium surrendered to the Nazis, and France was reeling under the German onslaught, being outmaneuvered and defeated at every turn. It was an extremely discouraging and frightening time.

On May 28 it all came to a head. Churchill met with his War Cabinet in a dingy room in the House of Commons during the afternoon, and a big discussion raged on whether Britain should fight or come to "terms" with Hitler and the Germans. Former Prime Minister Chamberlain and Lord Halifax, who had just recently turned down the opportunity to become Prime Minister,

---

[49] Churchill, *Never Give In!*, pp. 204-206.

did not support Churchill's position of wanting to fight the Germans' advance, and Churchill could not go forward without their support.

The Italian embassy, acting as a mediator for Hitler, had sent a message through Sir Robert Vansittart saying this was Britain's time to seek mediation. Churchill knew that if Britain accepted an offer of mediation that "the sinews of resistance would relax. A white flag would be invisibly raised over Britain, and the will to fight would be gone."[50] Churchill said no.

So Churchill left the meeting that afternoon, without the clear support of the War Cabinet, to go meet with the full cabinet. When he addressed the full cabinet, it was the first time many of them had heard him speak as Prime Minister.

This would be one of the most important speeches of his life. He began the speech calmly but ended with a climactic fervor that moved all in the room. He said,

> And I am convinced that every one of you would rise up and tear me down from my place if I were for one moment to contemplate parley or surrender. If this long island story of ours is to end at last, let it end only when each one of us lies choking in his own blood upon the ground.[51]

The response was powerful! The room came alive with men shouting and cheering, with some coming around and slapping him on the back.

"Churchill had ruthlessly dramatized and personalized the debate.

---

[50] Boris Johnson, *The Churchill Factor: How One Man Made History* (New York: Riverhead Books, 2014), pp. 11-13.
[51] Churchill, qtd. in Johnson, *The Churchill Factor*, p. 19.

When he returned to his War Cabinet meeting at 7 p.m. the debate was over! It was clear to all of them that he had the strong backing of the full cabinet. He had achieved a stunning victory. Britain would fight!"[52]

The news from the battlefield continued to worsen over the next week. On June 4, 1940, Churchill addressed the House of Commons again.

His speech that day was a long, detailed explanation of the situation on the mainland and what had recently transpired. He told about the totally unexpected Belgian surrender of their nearly 500,000 troops that left the Brits scrambling to cover their exposed flank to the sea, a distance of some 30 miles. That was the Brits only possible avenue of retreat.

He told the details of how the Navy and merchant seamen with some 1,100 vessels worked indefatigably under great duress and danger from the sea, the weather, and the enemy to rescue allies from the shores of the English Channel at Dunkirk, France. He told of the heroism and great accomplishments of the British Air Force that inflicted losses of 4 to 1 upon the Germans.

It had been a near miraculous escape for the Brits and the country was euphoric.

As Churchill spoke that day, he attempted to tamp down that euphoria a bit. He noted, "We must be very careful not to assign to this deliverance the attributes of a victory. Wars are not won by evacuations."[53]

Again Churchill demonstrated amazing leadership. Even though his nation had just barely avoided its largest military debacle since

---

[52] Johnson, *The Churchill Factor*, pp.18-19.
[53] Churchill, *Never Give In!*, p. 214.

1781 in the American War of Independence, his speech was indomitable!

> We shall go on to the end, we shall fight in France, we shall fight on the seas and oceans, we shall fight with growing confidence and growing strength in the air, we shall defend our Island, whatever the cost may be, we shall fight on the beaches, we shall fight on the landing grounds, we shall fight in the fields and in the streets, we shall fight in the hills; we shall never surrender, and even if . . . this Island or a large part of it were subjugated and starving, then our Empire beyond the seas, armed and guarded by the British Fleet, would carry on the struggle, until, in God's good time, the New World, with all its power and might, steps forth to the rescue and the liberation of the old.[54]

He was inspiring, resolute, determined! His speech motivated and stiffened the resolve of all.

Two weeks later he would give one of his most memorable speeches of all times. In a radio address on June 18, 1940, he said,

> Upon this battle depends the survival of Christian civilization. Upon it depends our own British life, and the long continuity of our intuitions and our Empire. The whole fury and might of the enemy must very soon be turned on us. Hitler knows that he will have to break us on this island or lose the war. If we can stand up to him all Europe may be free and the life of the world may move forward into broad, sunlit

---

[54] Churchill, *Never Give In! The Best of Winston Churchill's Speeches*, p. 218. This is from a speech on June 4, 1940.

uplands.

But if we fail, then the whole world, including the United States, including all we have known and cared for, will sink into the abyss of a new Dark Age made more sinister, and perhaps more protracted, by the lights of perverted science.

Let us therefore brace ourselves to our duties, and so bear ourselves that if the British Empire and its Commonwealth last for a thousand years, men will still say: "This was their finest hour."[55]

Winston Churchill 1941

Just four days later, France surrendered to Germany. Britain now stood alone. Churchill tried in vain to encourage continued French resistance to the Germans, but very little resistance materialized, a which was a very big disappointment to him. He continued his ongoing courtship with United States, trying to get them to enter the war. He believed strongly that if he could get the United States into the war the Allies could win. But this was an extremely hard sell. World War I had cost them more than 116,000 lives, and the Americans wanted no part of another bloody, grueling war in Europe.[56]

The German juggernaut continued to extend its domination. In

---

[55]William Manchester, *The Last Lion: Winston Spencer Churchill, Alone, 1932-1940* (Boston: Little, Brown and Company, 1988), p. 685. This perhaps his most famous speech, delivered on June 18, 1940, to the House of Commons.
[56] Defense Casualty Analysis System, U.S. Dept. of Defense, May 23, 2014.

April 1941 Germany invaded Greece and Yugoslavia. Both countries surrendered within three weeks.

Though at this time Britain stood alone against the Nazis, Churchill remained defiant! In a speech given in late October 1941 he was adamant in his resolve. He said,

> Never give in. Never, never, never, never—in nothing great or small, large or petty, never give in except to convictions of honor and good sense.
>
> > Never yield to force; never yield to the apparently overwhelming might of the enemy. We stood all alone a year ago, and to many countries it seemed that our account was closed, we were finished. . . . Very different is the mood today. [57]

The Americans would stay out of the war until their hand was finally forced, by the surprise Japanese attack on Pearl Harbor December 7, 1941. The next day, the United States declared war on Japan. Three days later on December 11, 1941, hours after Germany declared war on the United States the United States responded by declaring war on them.

The war raged for nearly four more years and resulted in the deaths of millions of people. It ended in Europe on May 7, 1945, with the unconditional surrender of all German forces to the allies. A few months later the Japanese would surrender after having atomic bombs dropped on two of their major cities.

In those early dark days of World War II, when Hitler's German army seemed unconquerable, as nation after nation fell to the

---

[57] Churchill, *Never Give In!*, p. 307. This speech was given on October 29, 1941, at Harrow School.

Nazis, one man, Winston Churchill, stood defiantly against overwhelming odds to challenge the inevitable—***When Leadership Mattered.***

His resolve, unflagging confidence and determination, inspired his nation to continue the fight until ultimate victory was achieved.

Bonus Notes

- In 1899 while serving as a journalist during the Second Boer War, Churchill was captured and imprisoned. This war was between the British Empire, the South Africa Republic, and the Orange Free State. These two states later incorporated into the Union of South Africa.

- After his daring escape from the Boers, he was celebrated as a hero and became a very successful and well-paid lecturer and author.

- Churchill became Prime Minister on May 10, 1940. In May and June Hitler's forces were rolling over Europe, and during that time Holland, Belgium, Norway, and France fell, one by one. Great Britain stood alone.

- Belgium unexpectedly surrendered on May 28, taking an army of 500,000 men out of the fight and leaving Britain's flank and their only route of possible escape, Dunkirk, exposed and vulnerable.

- To understand just how formidable Hitler's war machine was, we need to consider how long these nations were able to resist before surrendering: Denmark, 4 hours; Holland, 5 days; Yugoslavia, 12 days; Belgium, 18 days; Greece, 21 days; Poland, 27 days; and France, 6 weeks.

- As Prime Minister he wrote his own speeches and radio addresses, typically spending one hour of preparation for every minute he spoke.

- Churchill and Britain stood very much alone for nearly two years, from May 10, 1940, until Dec. 8, 1941, when the United States entered the war as an ally.

- Churchill suffered serious bouts of depression periodically for most of his life. He called his depression his "Black Dog." At times it affected his sleep, appetite, and ability to function.

- It's hard to understand that after rallying and saving his nation from Hitler's conquest, he was turned out of office as Prime Minister just two months after Germany's surrender.

CHAPTER SIX

William Wilberforce

The man who dedicated his life working to end the slave trade in England

By the late 1700s more than 11,000,000 African men, women, and children had been captured or bought to be sold as slaves primarily in the West Indies and to the American colonies. The loathsome practice of selling human beings into bondage was booming!

Great Britain, the great maritime nation and superpower of that time, was hugely involved in this extremely profitable slave trade. And, disappointing as it is to us today, the slave trade in that time was considered acceptable by most people.

William Wilberforce

But in 1789, a strong voice arose in the Parliament of Great Britain speaking out against the cruel and immoral slave trade. That voice was William Wilberforce, a young member of the Parliament. In that year he presented his first bill to abolish the slave trade—and was soundly defeated.

For nearly the next 20 years following that defeat, abolishing the British slave trade would be the primary focus and effort of his life. It would be an extremely formidable task, but he was determined to challenge the status quo.

William Wilberforce was only 30 years old when he took on this great work. A very diminutive man who stood only a little over 5 feet tall, he was an extremely witty person, a great orator, an engaging conversationalist, and a very talented singer.

He had turned many heads when he was elected to represent the district of Hull in the House of Commons at the age of 21, defeating Lord Manner and David Hartley. He garnered exactly as many votes as the two combined.

After serving in Parliament for four years, he took a trip with his mother, sister, and a few family members across the English Channel to France. He also invited a childhood friend, Isaac Milner, to come along for intelligent conversation.

Milner held the extremely prestigious chair of Lucasian Professor at Cambridge University. To confirm the esteemed level of this professorship, it can be noted that it was once held by Sir Isaac Newton and in modern times by Stephen Hawking.

At some point during the lengthy visit, he noticed a cousin's book on a table and picked it up. The book was *The Rise and Progress of Religion in the Soul* by Philip Doddridge.

He and Milner would read and discuss the book on the arduous 1,200-mile coach trip back, including 18 snowy days trekking over the French Alps and then the coast, and finally crossing the Channel to England. This book would propel him to embrace evangelical Anglicanism over a period of the next year and a half, dramatically changing his outlook and the direction of his life.

As his life turned more and more to God and matters of humanity, he strongly considered dropping out of politics and resigning his seat in Parliament. He discreetly sought the advice and spiritual counsel of John Newton.

As a youth he had often heard John Newton preach when he visited his aunt and uncle. Newton was a former slave ship captain who came to recognize the shame of his sin, had repented, and had turned to a life of service, preaching and writing hymns. One of his best known hymns is "Amazing Grace." Newton was in fact the only religious acquaintance that Wilberforce had.

Now, as a well-known member of Parliament, Wilberforce had to use clandestine methods to arrange a meeting with Newton. Had he been seen consorting with him, he could have been ostracized by family, friends, and political acquaintances. Spending time in the presence of Newton would get him labeled a "Methodist." In today's vernacular it would be the same as being called a "Bible thumper" or "holy roller."

Newton advised him to stay in Parliament despite the fact that others had suggested he drop out.

Wilberforce wrote to his dear friend William Pitt, who was the Prime Minister, about his spiritual awakening. He told him about the great change that had taken place in his life. He said that the change might have effects on his public conduct: "I told [Pitt] that although I should ever feel the greatest regard and affection for him, and had every reason to believe that I should in general be able to support his measures, I could no longer act as a party man."[58]

The close relationship between Pitt and Wilberforce had been formed while they were both students at Cambridge when Pitt's father, William Pitt the Elder, was the Prime Minister of England.

---

[58] Wilberforce, qtd. in Kevin Belmonte, *Hero for Humanity: A Biography of William Wilberforce* (Colorado Springs, CO: NavPress, 2002), p. 87.

The two enjoyed meeting often at the gallery in the House of Commons when visiting London. The friends spent countless hours watching and listening as lively debates raged below them. It was likely during this period that Wilberforce caught the political bug and decided to run for Parliament. Their friendship would be pivotal for both of them in the years to come.

Both men were extraordinarily gifted speakers, brilliant, charming, and witty. One significant difference between the two was that Pitt knew the nuances of politics: he had been around it his whole life, having been schooled and groomed by his father in the art of politics. His political savvy would play a pivotal role in Wilberforce's later success in getting the slave trade abolished.

Wilberforce's campaign to stop the slave trade was birthed in the first few months of 1787 when he began meeting with a group of abolitionists to discuss the issue and to exchange and update information with each other. In March of that year he first publicly announced to the group that he had decided to take up the cause of fighting for the abolition of the slave trade.

We can begin to understand the passion and determination that relentlessly drove Wilberforce to fight overwhelming odds to end this barbaric practice of buying and selling humans when we read the following account from Alexander Falconbridge, a ship's surgeon on a slave ship.

> The men Negroes on being brought aboard the ship, are immediately fastened together, two by two, by handcuffs on their wrists and irons riveted on their legs. . . . They are frequently stowed so close, as to admit no other position than lying on their sides. Nor will the height between decks, unless directly under the grating, permit the indulgence of an erect posture. . . .

They are far more violently affected by seasickness than Europeans. It frequently terminates in death, especially among the women. But the exclusion of fresh air is among the most intolerable. . . . The fresh air being thus excluded, the Negroes' rooms soon grow intolerable hot. The confined air, rendered noxious by the effluvia exhaled from their bodies and being repeatedly breathed, soon produces fevers and diarrhea which generally carries off great numbers of them. . . .

Some wet and blowing weather having occasioned the port-holes to be shut and the grating to be covered, (diarrheas) and fevers among the Negroes ensued. . . . The deck, that is the floor of their rooms, was so covered with the blood and mucus which had proceeded from them in consequence of the diarrhea that it resembled a slaughterhouse. It is not in the power of the human imagination to picture a situation more dreadful or disgusting.[59]

In May of 1787 at the urging of his good friend, William Pitt, now the Prime Minister, Wilberforce resolved to take up the cause to fight in the House of Commons for the abolition of the slave trade.

He gave notice in the House of Commons in late December that he intended to put forth the issue of abolishing the slave trade early in the next session. His plan was to present the bill in February, but he became very seriously ill with ulcerative colitis. His condition was so serious that several doctors thought that he would not live.

---

[59] Eric Metaxas, *Amazing Grace: William Wilberforce and the Heroic Campaign to End Slavery* (New York: Harper Collins, 2007), pp. 169-171.

By the following spring, March 1789, he was healthy enough to return to the House of Commons. On May 12 he gave a passionate speech lasting three hours calling for the abolition of the slave trade.

His speech was powerful and had great effect on the House. Edmund Burke stated that the speech "equaled anything he had heard in modern times, and was not, perhaps, to be surpassed in the remains of Grecian eloquence."[60]

However, despite eloquent speeches and strong support by some key allies for the abolition of the slave trade, the House of Commons voted to have a committee study the matter more thoroughly and to hear more in the next parliamentary session.

The next year Wilberforce succeeded in getting Parliament to form a select committee that would continue the process of gathering information both pro and con about the slave trade. But it would be the spring of 1791 before the debate resumed on the abolition of the slave trade.

Despite another valiant effort, the bill failed again. The vote was 88 for and 163 against.

In 1791 just days before his death, John Wesley, noted cleric and theologian, wrote a letter to Wilberforce giving strong encouragement and urging him to keep up his fight. Here is an excerpt from that letter.

> Dear Sir,
>
> Unless the divine power has raised you up to be as *Athanasius contra mundum* ["Athanasius against the world"], I see not how you can go

---

[60] Burke, qtd. In Belmonte, *Hero for Humanity*, p. 112.

through your glorious enterprise in opposing that
execrable villainy which is the scandal of
religion, of England, and of human nature.
Unless God has raised you up for this very thing,
you will be worn out by the opposition of men
and devils.

But if God be for you, who can be against you?
Are all of them stronger than God? O be not
weary of well doing. Go on, in the name of God
and in the power of His might, till even
American slavery (the vilest that ever saw the
sun) shall vanish before it.[61]

Wilberforce was a man of great religious conviction, which
strengthened him in the face of overwhelming opposition. Author,
Eric Metaxas notes,

Wilberforce prayed and read the Scriptures every
day, and he prayed with many others over these
issues and concerns. . . .

He also memorized lots of Scripture. In fact, he
memorized all of Psalm 119 and would recite it
on his daily 2 ½ mile walk to Parliament.[62]

The next year, April 2, 1792, Wilberforce again presented his bill
to abolish the slave trade. Again he made an impassioned speech
as did the Prime Minister, his friend, William Pitt.

Henry Dundas came up with a counter proposal that the slave trade

---

[61] John Wesley, "Letter to William Wilberforce," Feb. 24, 1791, in Thomas
Jackson, ed., *The Works of John Wesley*, vol. 13 (Franklin, TN: Providence
House, 1994), p. 153.
[62] Eric Metaxas, *Seven Men and the Secrets of their Greatness* (Nashville, TN:
Thomas Nelson, a 2014), p. 48.

not be abolished at once, but gradually. He proposed, and on April 27 the House of Commons agreed, that the slave trade would be abolished by January 1, 1796.

At first Wilberforce was greatly disappointed in the vote. However, as time went on he realized that a significant victory had been achieved, for it was the first time ever that the House had agreed to abolish the slave trade.

However, this victory was not to last. In February 1793 France and Britain went to war, and by late February the House refused to confirm the previous vote to gradually abolish slavery. The House was in no mood to debate the abolition issue while a savage war raged.

A period of great tumult and unrest ensued in Britain. The king was mobbed enroute to Parliament. Many commoners called for seizing the properties of the rich and redistributing wealth. Much anger was vented towards the rich, aristocratic landowners.

During this period Wilberforce supported bills that would greatly enhance the power of the government such as not allowing seditious assemblies. He, however, only supported these bills for a temporary period, feeling that they were necessary because of the threat being posed by revolutionary France. The fear was that revolution might be imported into Britain.

Wilberforce gave an impassioned, decisive speech to a gathering of thousands of his constituents and won them over to his and the government's side supporting the Treason and Sedition bills. His strong support helped his friend Prime Minister Pitt win this battle.

It wasn't long before Wilberforce was ready to once again try getting his abolition bill passed.

Meanwhile, the French had incited blacks in the English West

Indies; Grenada, Dominica, and St. Vincent to rebel against English authority. Some anti-abolitionists believed this type of rebellion was indicative of what Wilberforce and his abolitionist supporters intended.

With this backdrop, some supporters of the abolition movement encouraged Wilberforce to delay presenting his abolition bill until a more favorable time. Wilberforce disagreed.

On February 18, 1796, he introduced his abolition bill again. The bill made it through the first and second readings, but on the third reading the bill was defeated 74-70. Wilberforce was crushed.

It is interesting to note that the opposition had given free opera tickets to some of the supporters of the abolition bill, so some ten or twelve of the supporters were either at the opera or in the country for enjoyment, and missed this key vote.[63]

After the defeat Wilberforce was struck again by severe illness. He had a high fever and excruciating intestinal troubles. Though he was sick for several months he continued to work as much as he could. By May he was once again forced to campaign for reelection and won his seat on June 7.

In mid-July he wrote to his friend John Newton telling him he was considering retiring from public life. Newton encouraged him to stay the course saying, "Though you have not, as yet, fully succeeded in your persevering endeavors to abolish the slave trade, the business is still in [process]; and since you took it in hand, the condition of the slaves in our islands, has undoubtedly been already [improved]). . . . These instances to which others . . . might . . . be added, are proofs that you have not labored in vain."[64]

---

[63] Belmonte, Hero for Humanity, p. 134.
[64] Newton, qtd. in Belmonte, *Hero for Humanity*, p. 137.

Once again, at the urging of his old friend and spiritual advisor, he decided to stay in Parliament and continue to fight for the abolition of the slave trade.

For the next eleven years Wilberforce continued to persist in trying to get the abolition bill passed. From 1797 to 1799 his bill was defeated each year. No progress was made on the bill between the years 1800 to 1803 because of a feared French invasion.

William Pitt, Wilberforce's close friend and supporter, once again became Prime Minister in 1804 after being out of office for several years. He served until he died January 23, 1806, of complications resulting from severe gout. He was only 47 years old.

Lord Grenville then became Prime Minister. He was a solid supporter of the abolition bill and took steps to help Wilberforce secure passage.

A great irony is that Grenville and Charles James Fox, who at one time had been adversaries of Wilberforce, now became the two best allies in the drive to get the abolition bill passed.

Finally on the night of February 23, 1807 the tide turned for the "Abolition of the Slave Trade" bill. As the bill was debated, more and more of the speeches were in support of the bill. Excitement continued to build as members could sense the inevitability of the passage of the bill.

The climax of the night came when Solicitor General Sir Samuel Romilly closed his very moving speech by comparing Wilberforce and Napoleon and the reception each would receive upon arriving at home:

> Napoleon would arrive in pomp and power, a
> man who knew the height of earthly ambition,
> yet one tormented by bloodshed and the

oppressions of war. Wilberforce would come home to "the bosom of his happy and delighted family," able to lie down in peace because he had "preserved so many millions of his fellow creatures."[65]

The House of Commons rose to its feet, turned to Wilberforce, and began to cheer. They gave three rousing hurrahs while Wilberforce sat with his head bowed and wept. Then at 4 a.m., the Commons voted to abolish the slave trade by an overwhelming majority, 283 to 16.[66]

The fight to abolish the slave trade was over! It had taken nearly 20 years. The fact that Wilberforce had successfully orchestrated the change of attitude in the country and the Parliament on the issue of the slave trade in so short a time was incredible!

Wilberforce would be a champion for many humanitarian causes during his political career: child labor laws, prison reform, education reform, issues of public health, prevention of cruelty to animals, and others. But for nearly two decades he stood alone as the one man who challenged the status quo of the cruel, dehumanizing British slave trade. William Wilberforce, exhibiting great leadership, resolve, and courage, fought in the House of Commons until his battle to end the slave trade was won.

William Wilberforce was there—***When Leadership Mattered***.

---

[65] Belmonte, Hero for Humanity, p. 150
[66] Belmonte, *Hero for Humanity*, p. 148.

Bonus Notes

- As a youth Wilberforce was a small, sickly, boy with poor eyesight.

- Wilberforce was involved in many philanthropic and social causes. At one point he was active in 69 separate initiatives.

- He not only cared deeply for humans but also for animals. He was the founder of the Royal Society of Prevention of Cruelty to Animals.

- Sir James MacKintosh, a Scotsman, said this of Wilberforce: "If I were called upon to describe Wilberforce in one word, I would say he was the most 'amusable' man I ever met with in my life. Instead of having to think of what subjects will interest him it is perfectly impossible to hit one that does not. I never saw any one who touched life at so many points."[67]

- In a 1783 trip to Paris, Wilberforce, his friend William Pitt, and Edward Eliot met some of the most prominent people of that time including Benjamin Franklin, General Lafayette, Marie Antoinette, and Louis XVI.

- As he lay on his deathbed, three days before he died came the glorious news that Parliament had voted to outlaw slavery.

- Wilberforce is buried in Westminster Abby near his good friend, William Pitt.

---

[67] Quoted in John Piper, *Amazing Grace in the Life of William Wilberforce* (Wheaton, IL: Crossway, 2007), p. 60.

CHAPTER SEVEN

Abraham Lincoln

Through America's darkest hours he persevered to save the Union.

Considered by many to be one of the greatest presidents in United States history, Abraham Lincoln most likely could not get elected today! With a history of severe bouts of depression, melancholy, and two nervous breakdowns, he would be disqualified at the beginning of any campaign, deemed unfit to serve and mentally unstable.

With the possible exception of George Washington, no American president ever faced more daunting challenges during his presidency than Abraham Lincoln.

This chapter will focus on Lincoln's unique brand of leadership, why it was so important to our country from 1861-1865, and why his leadership mattered.

Situation

By the spring of 1861, the unrest and tensions that had smoldered in the country for decades over the issue of slavery and states' rights had erupted into a full scale war. The nation was ripped apart and in grave danger of becoming two divided nations forever.

As president in 1861, it fell to Lincoln to try to resolve these issues and save the Union. However, in order to solve the issue of slavery, states' rights, and many other divisive issues, he first had to win the war!

Without his specific leadership style and unique qualifications the war may well have been lost and the Union forever fractured.

Lincoln's Boyhood Years

It is worth looking at his background to understand what shaped Lincoln into the uniquely qualified man who could endure the incredible challenges he would face as president of a divided nation fighting a brutal civil war.

Certainly Lincoln's humble beginnings had a major role in shaping his life. Living part of his childhood in abject poverty, he learned early on how to survive hardship. For a part of his boyhood, he was as poor as or poorer than almost any slave in the South.

When his father, Thomas Lincoln, moved his family from Kentucky to the frontier of Indiana in 1816, they lived for a year in a three-sided hut with one side completely open. Young Abe and his sister slept on the ground on top of leaves and furs. A fire was kept burning night and day at the open side to heat the hut and to keep wild animals out. The conditions were squalid. They stayed dirty, ragged, and plagued by fleas, lice, and vermin. They subsisted mainly on wild game, wild fruit, and nuts. They ate with their fingers, as there were no eating utensils. To make matters worse, the winter of 1816-1817 was one of the coldest and most severe in the history of that region.

Lincoln's mother, Nancy, died from "milk sick" in 1818. This sickness was caused by consuming milk from cows that had eaten white snakeroot. She was only 35 years old.

After she died, Thomas built a cabin with 4 sides. It still had no floor, windows, or door except for a dirty bearskin.

He soon realized he desperately needed a wife, and his two children needed a mother. So, he left for Louisville, Kentucky, to court and find a wife. He left Sarah (12) and Abraham (10) untended and alone in the cabin on the prairie frontier for ten months while he was away.

Sarah Bush Johnston was a widow with three children, and she needed a husband probably as much as Thomas needed a wife. Thomas had courted and proposed to her 13 years earlier, but she had turned him down.

This time, she accepted. Once her debts were paid, they loaded up Thomas's wagon with her three children, Sarah Elizabeth (13), Matilda (10), and John D. Johnston (9), and off they rode to Indiana to their new home.

When she arrived with her children, life definitely got better for the Lincolns. Not only did she bring a table and chairs, pots and skillets, eating utensils, a walnut bureau, and a feather mattress and pillows, she brought order to the household. The squalid conditions ended as she had Thomas put in a floor and make beds and chairs. She cleaned the cabin and then kept it that way. Most importantly, she also gave love and encouragement to the children. Lincoln loved her dearly the rest of his life.

An Insatiable Desire to Learn

While Lincoln had little formal education, he and his sister attended school when he was 15 years old. They had to walk four miles each way to attend the school. All in all, he was able to attend school for about 12 months.

Lincoln always had an extremely strong desire to learn. He read every book he could get his hands on. "He read many hours in the family Bible, the only book in their cabin. He borrowed and read *Aesop's Fables, Pilgrim's Progress, Robinson Crusoe,* Grimshaw's *History of the United States, and* Weems's *The Life of George Washington, with Curious Anecdotes, Equally Honorable to Himself and Exemplary to His Young Countrymen.*"[68]

He also received his education in many ways outside of a classroom or the books he read. He once walked 30 miles to a courthouse so he could "hear lawyers speak and to see how they argued and acted. He heard roaring and ranting political speakers—and mimicked them. He listened to wandering evangelists who flung their arms and tore the air with their voices—and mimicked them."[69]

Lincoln as a young man

In 1831 Lincoln took a job on a flatboat taking pork, corn, and live hogs down river to New Orleans. Later that year he took a job as a clerk in New Salem, Illinois. He would go on to several other jobs becoming a partner in a grocery store, a postmaster, and a surveyor.

While he was a storekeeper, he bought a barrel of household goods from a traveler who was heading west and needed to lighten his load. Lincoln paid him 50 cents for the barrel without even examining its contents. Several weeks later he emptied the barrel to take inventory of what it contained. In the bottom of the barrel he found *Blackstone's Commentaries on the Law.* During the slow times in the store he began to read the four volumes. He became fascinated with these books on law and made the momentous decision to become a lawyer. This decision would set the course for his life. From this point on, he was continually borrowing and

---

[68] Carl Sandburg, *Abraham Lincoln: The Prairie Years and The War Years* (New York: Galahad Books, 1954), p. 14.
[69] Carl Sandburg, *Abraham Lincoln*, p. 15.

reading law books.

One of his proudest moments was being elected captain of the militia for the Black Hawk War. He only served four months and was never called on to fight but was none-the-less very proud of his service.

He ran unsuccessfully for the Illinois Legislature in 1832. In 1834 he was elected and would be reelected in 1836, 1838, and 1840.

Lincoln received his law license in 1836. His good humor and the ability to tell homespun yarns helped him become a very successful lawyer.

The highlight and the low point of his life was falling in love with Ann Rutledge, the love of his life. When she tragically became sick and died of typhoid, he was devastated and grieved terribly. He would walk five miles each day to Concord Cemetery where he would sit by her grave for hours. Lincoln's friends were so concerned about his depression they took his pocket knife away from him, fearing he would harm himself.

According to his lawyer friend William Herndon, "From the day of Ann's death he was a changed individual. The melancholy that settled upon him lifted at times for short intervals; but it grew steadily worse, until he became the saddest man in Illinois." Herndon, later his law partner, said, "If Lincoln ever had a happy day in twenty years, I never knew of it. . . . Melancholy dripped from him as he walked." [70]

Lincoln would suffer from bouts of deep depression and melancholy for the rest of his life.

---

[70] Herndon, qtd. in Dale Carnegie, *Lincoln the Unknown* (Hauppauge, NY: Dale Carnegie & Associates, 1932), p. 45.

Mary Todd

In March of 1837 Lincoln left New Salem and moved to Springfield. He didn't have a lot of money or friends, and he only spoke to one woman in a year. But in 1839 that changed. A young woman by the name of Mary Todd had become angry with her stepmother, left her father's house in Kentucky, and went to live with her married sister in Springfield.

Mary, according to many accounts, had a high and haughty manner along with a volatile temper. She had been taught to speak French (with a Parisian accent) and could dance the Cotillion and the Circassion Circle. Her strong conviction was that she would marry a man who would become president of the United States. She boasted that she was determined to be First Lady and live in the White House.

As it happened, she couldn't have lived in a place better for her to possibly fulfill her desire to marry well. Springfield, Illinois, was home for two ambitious young men who had aspirations for high office, Stephen A. Douglas and Abraham Lincoln. Mary ended up being courted by both of them and supposedly entertained proposals from each. They would both run for president in the 1860 election.

When asked which one of her suitors she intended to marry she said, "Him which has the best prospects of being president."[71]

Lincoln did very well with his law practice in Springfield. By the time of his marriage to Mary Todd in 1842, he was earning as much as the governor, about $1,200 per year.

He served in Congress from 1847-1849. This period was dominated by controversies concerning the Mexican War. His

---

[71] Mary Todd, qtd. in Dale Carnegie, *Lincoln the Unknown*, p. 52.

position against the war was very unpopular in Illinois, so much so that some Democratic newspapers said he had committed political suicide.[72]

Lincoln Becomes a National Figure

In 1858 Lincoln ran for the United States Senate against Stephen A. Douglas, the well-known and highly respected senator from Illinois. The two captured the national spotlight during their much heralded Lincoln-Douglas debates. The debates drew thousands of spectators to each of the seven events and were covered extensively in newspapers around the country. Their campaign became the focal point of the raging national argument about the issue of slavery.

Even though Lincoln won more popular votes, the election was decided in the Illinois legislature. Lincoln lost.

The Highly Volatile Election of 1860

In the highly contentious presidential election of 1860 Lincoln won the election, but he did not win a majority of the votes. The Democrat Party was split in two with a Northern wing that voted for Stephen A. Douglas and a Southern faction which favored John C. Breckinridge. Additionally, there was a fourth candidate, John Bell of the newly formed Constitution Party.

While Lincoln received only 40% of the popular votes, not even a simple majority, he did convincingly win the electoral votes. He won 180, Douglas only won 12 even though he had gotten the second most popular votes, Breckinridge received 72, and John Bell won 39 electoral votes. It is worth noting that Lincoln did not receive a single vote from nine of the eleven Southern states that

---

[72] James M. McPherson, *Abraham Lincoln* (New York: Oxford University Press, 2009), p. 14.

would ultimately secede from the union—not one single vote!

Pre-inauguration

Before he was inaugurated on March 4, 1861, representatives from seven of those Southern states had already met at Montgomery, Alabama, seceded from the union, elected Jefferson Davis as the president, and formed the Confederate States of America.

Lincoln left his home in Springfield, Illinois, on February 11 enroute to Washington for his inauguration on a planned 12-day trip with numerous public stops and speeches. Friends, however, urged him to forgo his public schedule and slip into Washington unannounced. This was because of dozens of threatening letters and a plot to assassinate him that had been uncovered by the Secret Service and private detectives. So after making a speech in Harrisburg, Pennsylvania, on February 22, he slipped out the back door of a hotel, disguised so as to be unrecognizable, and made his way by train to Philadelphia where he had to change trains. Once again he disguised himself and was snuck onto a train bound for Washington where he arrived in secret.

He may have arrived safely, but he faced a torrent of criticism. Even the Republican-friendly *New York Tribune* excoriated him. They opined that this was "the only instance in recorded history in which the recognized head of a nation . . . has been compelled, for fear of his life, to enter the capital in disguise"; *The Charleston Mercury* slammed him saying, "Everybody here is disgusted at this cowardly and undignified entry.".[73] In the next few days illustrated newspapers began ridiculing him with cartoons of him wearing a variety of disguises, none flattering.

---

[73] *Lincoln in "The Times": The Life of Abraham Lincoln as originally reported in the "New York Times,"* eds. David Herbert Donald and Harold Holzer (New York: St. Martin's Press, 2005), p. 66.

Inauguration

General Winfield Scott, Commander-in-Chief of the Army, fearing that Lincoln would be shot during the inauguration ceremony, posted sixty soldiers beneath the platform from which Lincoln spoke. He also had soldiers on guard in the Capitol behind the president and many more soldiers encircling the audience to his front.

After the ceremony Lincoln rode in a carriage down Pennsylvania Avenue with green-coated snipers on rooftops and rows of infantry soldiers with bristling bayonets along the street. It was not a normal beginning. No one could have imagined what a challenging, tumultuous, and bloody four years lay ahead for the nation.

War!

Abraham Lincoln, 1863

Lincoln had barely a month in office before he was faced with an all-out open rebellion. Fort Sumter, South Carolina, still in Federal hands, was a thorn in the side of the newly formed Confederacy. They demanded that the fort and all other federal property within their borders be turned over to them immediately.

Lincoln and his Cabinet anguished over whether or not to resupply the fort and show firm resolve or turn it over to the South and hopefully prevent or at least delay war. Their hand was forced when rebel forces led by General P. G. T. Beauregard demanded its surrender and were rebuffed.

At 4:30 a.m. on April 12, 1861, the Confederate attack began. For nearly two full days the rebels fired more than 3,000 cannon shot and shells. The masonry fort took a tremendous pounding. The great fear of Major Robert Anderson, the Union commander, was that an incendiary shell would hit the magazine where their powder and shells were stored and blow them all to bits.

Finally, the white flag of surrender was hoisted and the fort fell. Almost miraculously, no lives had been lost in the bombardment. One Union soldier had died in an accident.

Probably no opening salvo in any war was ever so misleading as the absence of deaths in this battle. Before the final shots were fired four years later, more than 620,000 Americans would die in this bloody Civil War that pitted North against South, American against American, and sometimes even brother against brother.

On April 15, just a few days after the battle at Fort Sumter, Lincoln issued a call for 75,000 militia to quell the rebellion. Immediately four more states seceded.

Four days later Lincoln initiated a naval blockade of the Confederate coastline and southern ports. This was a bold and massive undertaking. It meant the U.S. Navy would have to blockade and patrol about 3,500 miles of coastline and twelve major ports. It was necessary because much of the South's arms, munitions, and war supplies would come in by ship.

A few months later found Union and Confederate armies moving toward the important rail center of Manassas, Virginia, or Bull Run, as it was called by the Confederates. It was late July 1861, and the mood in Washington was buoyant. Most people expected that with one good fight the rebels could be licked, and the war would be over.

Crowds of congressmen, their ladies and others drove out some 25 miles from Washington to Manassas in their fancy carriages with picnic baskets on hand to watch what promised to be a great show. The spectators were not prepared for what was about to happen.

Instead of a pleasant, orderly spectacle, a bloody battle developed. For several hours it was pretty much an even fight. And then, the battle changed. The Federals' advance stalled, giving the Confederates time to reorganize and reform their lines. About 4 p.m. fresh Confederate troops arrived and assaulted the Union lines on Chinn Ridge. The exhausted Federals began to fall back. At first it was an orderly withdrawal. But because the road to the rear was jammed with carriages and spectators, it was almost impassable. A panic started and soon the withdrawal became a full scale rout. Union soldiers fled and soon an all-out debacle ensued. Equipment was abandoned, many soldiers threw down their muskets, and a mad race began back toward Washington, or anywhere, to get away from the rebels.

As the smoke cleared from this first major battle of the war, the realization dawned on many that this could turn into a long and bloody war.

Examples of His Leadership

The Civil War and a nation in complete turmoil would require Lincoln to use every bit of wisdom, political savvy, patience, and humility he could muster to succeed as president. Fortunately, he was a humble man and, seemingly, unfazed by insults. This paid off for him as he was able to turn political rivals into team members. One remarkable example of this was Edwin Stanton. He detested Lincoln! He had called him a "painful imbecile" and declared that "he was utterly incapable of running the government and that he ought to be ousted by a military dictator."[74]

---

[74] Carnegie, *Lincoln the Unknown*, p. 154.

After only ten months in office, Lincoln's administration was rocked with scandal. Profiteers were robbing the government of millions of dollars through dishonest war contracts. Lincoln looked beyond the insults he knew Stanton had flung at him and took the high road. Knowing that Stanton was a tiger and had the mental toughness needed for that job, Lincoln appointed him as the Secretary of War. That position was one of the most influential and powerful jobs in the Administration. Stanton was tenacious and did a fantastic job! It was said to be one of the best appointments Lincoln made while in office.

A valuable lesson here is that great leaders recognize outstanding abilities, even in a foe, and strive to make them a part of the team and not an adversary.

Another crucial decision Lincoln faced as a wartime president was determining who could best lead his Army to victory. When Lincoln fired General George B. McClellan as commander of the Army of the Potomac, he stunned the nation. It was "entirely unexpected to all," said the report in the *New York Times*.[75]

McClellan was very popular and well-respected. His troops loved him. The only problem was he wouldn't fight. Even though he always outnumbered Lee, he was continually calling for more reinforcements and making excuses about why he wasn't attacking. Lincoln caustically called the Army of the Potomac, "McClellan's body-guard."[76] After the Battle of Antietam, Lincoln visited him at his camp and strongly urged him to move. Nothing happened. He then ordered McClellan to advance.

Lincoln reports that "It was 19 days before he put a man across the river. It was 9 days more before he put his army across and then

---

[75] Donald and Holzer, eds., *Lincoln in "The Times,"* p. 154.
[76] Paul M. Zall, ed., *Lincoln on Lincoln* (Lexington: University Press of Kentucky, 1999) p. 133.

he stopped again, delaying on little pretexts of wanting this and that. I began to fear he was playing false—that he did not want to hurt the enemy. I saw how he could intercept on the way to Richmond. I determined to make that the test. If he let them get away I would remove him. He did so and I relieved him."[77]

In this situation, Lincoln showed great boldness and conviction. He knew he needed to make a change in the leadership and direction of the Army—and he did! A strong leader is capable of making the tough decisions when needed, even if it's not a popular decision.

Though he always sought and listened to the recommendations made by his Cabinet and his generals, Lincoln made the hard decisions himself. For example, the decision to issue the Emancipation Proclamation in January 1863 to free the slaves in the rebel states was his and his alone. (A seldom mentioned fact is that the Emancipation Proclamation did not free the slaves that were still held in the four Union states of Kentucky, Indiana, Delaware, and Missouri.)

Lincoln's Emancipation Proclamation was a bold step and allowed him to seize the moral high ground by freeing the slaves. This move helped persuade England and France to stay out of the war. There had been a great fear in the North that they would come in on the side of the Confederacy in order to protect their interest in keeping Southern cotton available for their textile mills.

Another example of Lincoln's leadership was that he allowed his generals to lead (if they would) without his interference. A great example of this took place regarding General William T. Sherman and his decision to march from Atlanta to the sea. It was believed by many that this was a very risky proposition because Sherman

---

[77] Lincoln, qtd. in Zall, ed., *Lincoln on Lincoln*, p. 172.

and his army were deep in enemy territory and far beyond his supply lines.

After the success of that march, Lincoln said in a letter to General Sherman in December 1864, "I was anxious, if not fearful; but feeling that you were the better judge, and remembering 'that nothing risked, nothing gained' I did not interfere. Now the undertaking being a success, the honor is all yours. . . . But what next? I suppose it will be safer if I leave Gen. Grant and yourself to decide."[78]

One of Lincoln's strongest leadership qualities was his absolute focus and single-mindedness about preserving the Union—no matter what.

As a young lawyer, he had a knack for focusing on the main issue. It was said he would give away six points and carry the seventh and win the case.[79]

To get a better understanding on exactly how single-minded or focused he was on this issue, we can read his response to an editorial written by Horace Greeley in the *National Intelligencer* on August 20, 1862.

Lincoln's Position on Freeing Slaves, August 23, 1862

> My paramount object in this struggle is to save the Union, and is not either to save or destroy slavery. If I could save the Union without freeing any slaves I would do it, and if I could save it by freeing all the slaves I would do it; and if I could save it by freeing some and leaving others alone, I would also do that. What I do about slavery, and the colored race, I do because I believe it helps to save the

---

[78] Lincoln, qtd. in Zall, ed., *Lincoln on Lincoln*, p. 163.
[79] McPherson, *Abraham Lincoln*, p. 12.

Union; and what I forbear, I forbear because I do not believe it would help save the Union. I shall do less whenever I shall believe what I am doing hurts the cause, and I shall do more whenever I shall believe doing more will help the cause. I shall try to correct errors when shown to be errors; and I shall adopt new views so fast as they shall appear to be true views. I have here stated my purpose according to my view of official duty; and I intend no modification of my oft-expressed personal view that all men, everywhere could be free.[80]

As situations and often the facts would change, he was not averse to changing his mind or position on things. As we read the letter above, we can see his mind, his mission (and seemingly) his only goal was to preserve the Union, not free the slaves. Yet four months later, January 1, 1863, he would issue the Emancipation Proclamation.

Lincoln faced harsh political infighting within his own party and even within his own Cabinet, four of whom had been political rivals in the presidential campaign of 1860.

"Almost every man in the Cabinet considered himself superior to Lincoln. After all, who was this crude, awkward, story-telling Westerner they were supposed to serve under? A political accident, a 'dark horse' that had got in by chance and crowded them out." [81]

Lincoln cared deeply about every citizen and soldier, and he showed it by the incredible effort he made to meet citizens and visit the troops and commands. Every day hundreds of people visited him in the White House. He would see every person who waited to see him. He also made it a point to often visit soldiers around Washington and at battlefields in Virginia and Maryland.

---

[80] Lincoln, qtd. in Zall, ed., *Lincoln on Lincoln*, p. 131.
[81] Dale Carnegie, *Lincoln the Unknown*, p. 148.

He visited troops eleven times and spent forty-two days with the Army.[82] He would visit the wounded and shake hundreds of hands every day. He once spent six hours on horseback reviewing the troops of McClellan's army.

He took time to think things through. He was a slow, methodical thinker and slow to respond. He often wrote letters and then did not send them. One famous example was the letter he penned to General George G. Meade who won the most significant battle of the war at Gettysburg. Under his leadership his forces inflicted staggering losses on General Robert E. Lee's army. Some of Lee's units, such as General George Pickett's division, suffered almost unbelievable 50 percent casualties of its total strength during the famous "Pickett's Charge" on the third and final climactic day at Gettysburg.

But instead of capitalizing on the success of the three-day battle, Meade did not pursue Lee. As Lee retreated, his army was blocked from crossing the flooded Potomac River and was extremely vulnerable. Meade might well have ended the war then and there had he kept pressure on Lee's badly mauled army. But he didn't, and they crossed the river and got away. Soon they had licked their wounds, reorganized, and were a formidable force again.

Lincoln was bitterly disappointed in Meade's lost opportunity, and he wrote a very cryptic letter to him on July 14: "Again, my dear general, I do not believe you appreciate the magnitude of the misfortune involved in Lee's escape. He was within your easy grasp, and to have closed upon him would, in connection with our other late successes [the surrender of Vicksburg and Port Hudson on the Mississippi River, along with their 36,000 defenders], have ended the war. As it is, the war will be prolonged indefinitely. . . .

---

[82] McPherson, *Abraham Lincoln*, p. 35.

Your golden opportunity is gone."[83]

Meade's failure to pursue and destroy Lee's army when he had such a great advantage and opportunity was indicative of what nearly all Lincoln's commanding generals did. Lincoln went through a litany of generals during the war; Brigadier General Irvin McDowell, General George B. McClellan (twice), General Ambrose E. Burnside, General "Fighting Joe" Hooker, and finally Meade. Unfortunately for Lincoln, even though the Union forces had superiority in numbers of men, equipment, weapons, ammunition, ample food, wagons, tents, uniforms, etc., while the Confederates were ragged, poorly fed, and almost always outnumbered, no Union general would press the attack on Lee's army.

Federal commanders who would fight Lee, usually on ground of his choosing, were usually beaten or badly punished and would end up withdrawing or retreating. Not until Lincoln appointed General Ulysses S. Grant to be General-in-Chief of all Union Armies did the tide change. In Grant he found a fighter—a general who would use his advantage in men and material and relentlessly press Lee's army in a bloody war of attrition that would ultimately cause the defeat of the Confederate forces.

If fighting a great Civil War wasn't enough to tax his leadership, he also faced the New York Draft Riots in July, 1863, the largest civil insurrection in the nation's history! Three days of violence resulting in the deaths of 100 people and the destruction of millions of dollars' worth of property. The rioters were newly arrived Irish-Americans who were unwilling to be drafted and sent to the bloody battlefields to fight to abolish slavery. Union soldiers who had recently faced General Lee's army at Gettysburg now had to be brought to New York City to bear arms against

---

[83] Lincoln, qtd. in Zall, ed., *Lincoln on Lincoln*, pp. 141-142.

newly arrived immigrants who refused to be conscripted into the army.

And, in the midst of it all, Lincoln had to run for re-election for president in 1864. His opponent was his former slow-moving army commander, George B. McClellan. He handily defeated him.

But through all his challenges, he persevered! He successfully executed the war and then set a positive tone for Reconstruction.

Lincoln possessed great political skill and savvy. No one has done a better job than noted author James M. McPherson, of describing the daunting minefield that Lincoln had to navigate as President during the Civil War. He wrote:

> Only after years of studying the powerful crosscurrents of political and military pressures on Lincoln did I come to appreciate the skill with which he steered between the numerous shoals of conservatism and radicalism, free states and slave states, abolitionists, Republicans, Democrats, and border state Unionists to maintain a steady course that brought the nation to victory—and the abolition of slavery—in the end. If he had moved decisively against slavery in the war's first year, as radicals pressed him to do, he might well have fractured his war coalition, driven border-state Unionists over to the Confederacy, lost the war, and witnessed the survival of slavery for at least another generation.[84]

But most importantly, Abraham Lincoln was successful in preserving the Union! The only way that could be accomplished was to win the war. No compromises, no treaties, no agreements between the belligerents would ever have been able to do that.

---

[84] McPherson, *Abraham Lincoln*, p. x.

Lincoln believed that "the central idea pervading this struggle is the necessity that is upon us, of proving that popular government is not an absurdity. We must settle this question now, whether in a free government the minority have the right to break up the government whenever they choose. [85]

He feared that "if one state may secede at will, so may any other until there is no government and no nation."[86]

At his famous Gettysburg Address he succinctly laid the issue out when he said, "Now we are engaged in a great Civil War testing whether that nation or any nation so conceived and so dedicated can long endure."

And, winning the war was no small task. It would take every bit of skill, courage, tact, strong leadership ability, and divine help to see it through to the end.

Conclusion

In our nation's darkest hour, the four years of the Civil War, one man was determined that the Union, our United States of America, would survive. Even though the nation was wracked with a bloody war that cost more than 620,000 dead and tens of thousands wounded, many having lost limbs, with untold millions of dollars in property destroyed, cities burned, railroads wrecked, fields untended, animosity and hatred that would last for generations, he persevered. He was attacked, ridiculed, slandered, vilified, hated—but he stayed the course.

He made the tough decisions, did what was necessary to win a brutal war to hold the Union together, and began the process of reunification that preserved the United States of America.

---

[85] Lincoln, qtd. in McPherson, *Abraham Lincoln*, p. 34.
[86] Lincoln, qtd. in McPherson, *Abraham Lincoln*, p. 34.

When Lincoln lay dying in the house across the street from Ford Theatre where he had been shot, Secretary of War Edwin Stanton, the man who had once called him a "painful imbecile" now said, "There lies the most perfect ruler of men the world has ever seen."[87]

In a time of war, division, hate, and turmoil, Abraham Lincoln preserved the union and kept our nation intact—***When Leadership Mattered.***

Bonus Notes

- Honest Abe. When his general store in New Salem failed, a $1,100 debt was owed. Since he was only part-owner, Lincoln was only required by law to pay one half of the debt, but instead he paid it all. It took him fourteen years to pay it off! He called it his "national debt." Out of this period, he earned the reputation and the enduring nickname "Honest Abe."[88]

- On January 1, 1841, Lincoln was a NO-SHOW for his wedding to Mary Todd!

- On November 4, 1842 after a very interesting reconciliation and courtship, he proposed (again) to Mary Todd. She insisted that they get married that very day. They did! The wedding cake was still warm from the oven. She was taking no chances of him changing his mind this time!

- While today we think of Lincoln as distinguished, stately, etc., that was not always the perception folks had. In 1854

---

[87] Stanton, qtd. in Dale Carnegie, *Lincoln the Unknown*, p. 156.
[88] McPherson, *Abraham Lincoln*, p. 5.

when he was scheduled to give a speech at the State Fair in Springfield, his wife Mary had gone to extra effort that morning to make sure he was cleaned up and presented a neat appearance. But, by the time he appeared to speak, he wasn't wearing a coat or his vest, didn't have his collar on, and was without a tie. His shirt hung loosely, his hair was disheveled, his boots were dirty, and he only had one gallis (suspender) holding up his too-short, ill-fitting trousers.

- After the famous Lincoln-Douglas debates for the U.S. Senate which garnered national attention and huge crowds, Lincoln decided that he would make the most of his fame and earn some money by giving lectures. He rented a lecture hall in Bloomington, Illinois, and stationed a young lady at the door to sell tickets. Not one single person came—not one![89]

- A couple of months before the Republican Convention (at which he would receive the presidential nomination), the editor of the *Philadelphia Press* wrote a lengthy feature article listing the top forty-five men who were contenders for the nomination. Abraham Lincoln was not even mentioned![90]

- Lincoln was so sure that he wouldn't be nominated, he didn't even go to the Republican Convention like the other 40,000 folks who flooded into Chicago for the tumultuous event. He was at home working in his law office in Springfield, Illinois. Anxious to hear news from the Convention he wandered over to the *Springfield Journal*

---

[89] Carnegie, *Lincoln the Unknown*, p. 107.
[90] Gene Griessman and Pat Williams, with Peggy Matthews Rose, *Lincoln Speaks to Leaders: 20 Powerful Lessons for Today's Leaders from America's 16th President* (Charleston, SC: Elevate, 2009), p. 102.

newspaper office which had a telegraph wire. "He was sitting in a big arm-chair, discussing the second ballot, when suddenly the [telegraph] operator burst down the stairway, crying: 'Mr. Lincoln, you are nominated! You are nominated!'[91] He, and most other folks, were amazed. No one thought he had a chance!

- All of Lincoln's relatives on his father's side and all but one on his mother's side voted against him for president. They were Democrats.

- In the presidential election of 1860 Lincoln did not receive one vote, not one, in nine Southern states!

- Because of the fear of grave robbers and some other considerations, Lincoln's remains were moved seventeen times! He finally ended up in Springfield, Illinois, in 1901 (thirty-six years after his death). His remains are buried 6 feet beneath the floor of his tomb and are encased in a great ball of steel and concrete.[92]

---

[91] Carnegie, *Lincoln the Unknown*, pp. 111-112.
[92] Carnegie, *Lincoln the Unknown*, p. 252.

CHAPTER EIGHT

Susan B. Anthony

A Pioneer for Women's Right to Vote

It's hard to imagine a time in America when roughly one half of its citizens did not possess the basic rights of citizenship. Women could not vote and could not go to college or become doctors, ministers, or elected representatives. They had no control of their earnings and no claim to property; they were not allowed to speak in public forums and were not even allowed to order their own food in a restaurant.

The types of jobs or professions available to them consisted mainly of working in factories, sewing, housework, or teaching. This was the plight of women in America the year that Susan Brownell Anthony was born.

Anthony would become the most prominent leader in the fight for women's rights—especially the right to vote. She co-founded the National American Women's Suffrage Association in 1869 and led it as president for the next thirty-seven years.

Anthony was born on February 15, 1820, in Adams, Massachusetts. Her father, the owner of a cotton mill, was a religious man who taught his children to show their love for God by working to help other people.

She grew up in the Quaker or Friends religion. At the Friends Meeting House, women and men were treated as equals; everyone could speak without reservation, something that was extremely rare in the mid-1800s. Anthony attended a boarding school in Philadelphia, Pennsylvania. However, in 1837 she was forced to leave when her father's growing debt forced him to sell his business and move the family to a farm near Rochester, New York. She became a teacher and continued to teach until 1849, when her father asked her to come home to run the family farm while he spent more time trying to develop an insurance business.

While living at her father's home, Anthony was influenced by many famous reformers of the day—men such as Frederick Douglass, William Lloyd Garrison, and Wendell Phillips who were all visitors to her father's home. Their discussions and conversations helped her form some of her strong views on women's rights, slavery, and temperance (the limiting or avoidance of alcohol).

While Anthony's family attended the first women's rights convention in 1848 held in Seneca Falls and Rochester, New York, she personally did not take up the cause until 1851. She had devoted most of her time and effort until that time to the temperance movement.

The Spark That Caused Her to Fight for Women's Equal Rights

She made the pivotal decision to begin working for women's rights when male members of the temperance movement refused to let her speak at a rally simply because she was a woman.

She was attending a Sons of Temperance meeting in Albany, New York, as a duly appointed representative of the Rochester Daughters of Temperance. "The Convention accepted her credentials and seated her, but when she tried to 'speak to a motion,' the president told her 'the sisters were not invited to speak but to listen and learn.'"[93]

This confirmed to her that women had to have the right to speak in public and vote before they could make significant impact and really get things done. She left the conference immediately.

Her lifelong friendship and partnership with Elizabeth Cady Stanton (1815–1902), who had proposed a resolution giving women the right to vote, also began in 1851.

Anthony's commitment to women's rights was further strengthened when she attended her first women's rights convention in 1852. From that time until the end of the Civil War in 1865, she campaigned vigorously for women's rights and the abolition of slavery. Her campaign was tirelessly waged door to door, in meetings and in legislatures.

While traveling in New York she had an experience that opened her eyes to the injustice of wives having absolutely no control of their own money. Even if a woman worked, legally, the wages belonged to the husband. She recounted an event that happened in New York when she and another woman lecturer were traveling through the state in the harsh winter of 1854.

> We stopped at a little tavern where the landlady was not yet twenty and had a baby fifteen months old. Her supper dishes were not washed and her baby was crying, but she was equal to the occasion. She rocked the little thing to sleep, washed the dishes and got our supper; beautiful white bread, butter, cheese, pickles, apple and mince pie, and excellent peach preserves. She gave us her warm bedroom to sleep in, and on a row of pegs hung the

---

[93] Elizabeth Frost-Knappman and Kathryn Cullen-DuPont, *Women's Suffrage in America: An Eyewitness History* (New York: Oxford University Press, 1992), p. 96.

loveliest embroidered petticoat and baby clothes, all the work of that young woman's fingers, while on a rack was her ironing perfectly done, wrought undersleeves, baby dresses, embroidered underwear, etc. She prepared a 6 o'clock breakfast for us, at my special request, a plate of delicious baked sweet apples and a pitcher of rich milk. Now for the moral of this story: When we came to pay our bill, the dolt of a husband took the money and put it in his pocket. He had not lifted a hand to lighten that woman's load, but had sat and talked with the men in the bar room, not even caring for the baby, yet the law give him the right to every dollar she earns, and when she needs two cents to buy a darning needle she has to ask him and explain what she wants it for. [94]

A few years later this type of situation was largely remedied by the passage of the New York State Married Women's Property and Guardianship Law in 1860. This law that gave married women in New York greater property rights was Anthony's first major legislative victory.

Arrested for Voting!

In 1872 the presidential race was between Ulysses S. Grant and Horace Greeley. Susan B. Anthony gained national attention and notoriety when she and fifteen supporters from Rochester showed up at the polls and became the first women ever to vote in a presidential election. They were promptly arrested!

The arrest did not deter Anthony. She was eager to test women's legal right to vote under the Fourteenth Amendment and hoped to take the case to the U.S. Supreme Court.

---

[94] Lynn Sherr, *Failure Is Impossible: Susan B. Anthony in Her Own Words*, Lynn Sherr (New York: Random House, 1995), p. 47.

She was unable to testify in her own behalf since she was a woman. She lost her case in 1873 in Rochester following some questionable rulings by the judge and was barred from appealing the result to the Supreme Court. She was fined $100 which she refused to pay. She campaigned throughout the country with a carefully prepared legal argument entitled "Is It a Crime for a U.S. Citizen to Vote?"

Later Years

Susan B. Anthony spent the rest of her life working for the federal

Susan B. Anthony

suffrage amendment and other women's rights—an exhausting job that took her not only to Congress but to political conventions, labor meetings, and lecture halls in every part of the country. She traveled extensively, giving 75 to 100 speeches each year. She addressed every Congress from 1869 until the year of her death in 1906.

In about the mid-1870s she noticed that most historical literature did not mention any women at all, so in 1877 she and some of her supporters sat down to begin writing the *History of Woman Suffrage* in six volumes. Later she worked with her biographer, Ida Husted Harper, on two of the three volumes of *The Life and Work of Susan B. Anthony*. The material was drawn mainly from the scrapbooks she had kept throughout most of her life. These materials—her scrapbooks, diaries, and letters—are now in the Library of Congress.

Anthony stayed active in the struggle for women's suffrage until the end of her life. She attended her last suffrage convention in February, 1906, just one month before her death.

At the time of her death on March 13, 1906, only four states had granted women the right to vote. Fourteen years later the Nineteenth Amendment, which gave women the right to vote, was added to the U.S. Constitution.

There have been numerous efforts by the federal government to honor her. These efforts include the Susan B. Anthony dollar coin that was introduced in 1979 with much fanfare. Unfortunately the dollar coin was not widely accepted because it had the same look and feel as a 25-cent piece.

Other efforts to recognize and honor Anthony were a marble statue in the crypt of the U.S. Capitol. The statue also included her colleagues in the women's rights movement, Elizabeth Cady Stanton and Lucretia Mott.

Anthony was also featured on two postage stamps, one in 1936 and another in 1955. Her home in Rochester, New York, became a national historic landmark in 1966.

Conclusion

After her death in 1906 a newspaper columnist wrote the following: "Her career illustrates again what a life devoted to a single idea can accomplish—how much of dynamics there is in actually knowing, not merely believing, that you are right."[95]

Anthony helped change the course of history in the United States through her efforts to enable women to vote. She helped change both minds and laws. Without her total devotion and tireless efforts in organizing, lecturing, lobbying, and campaigning for

---

[95]Quoted in Sherr, *Failure Is Impossible*, p. xx.

change, a woman's right to vote and fully participate in the Republic could have been many more years in coming.

In her last public speech she said, "Failure is impossible."[96]

Her boldness, tenacity, and steadfast devotion to the cause of women's rights changed America for the better.

Susan B. Anthony was there in the fight for women's rights and equality—***When Leadership Mattered***.

Bonus Notes

- Hooted down at her first public meeting, she went on to become one of the most popular lecturers of her day.

- Anthony helped changed not only the attitudes but the laws to ensure equal rights for women.

- She possessed tremendous energy and endurance even in her later years. At the age of 75 she toured Yosemite National Park on the back of a mule.

- Anthony had several offers of marriage in her later years, but there is no record of her ever having a serious romance.

- She was the first woman to have her likeness appear on a United States coin, the 1979 Susan B. Anthony dollar.

- Anthony celebrated her 80th birthday in the White House at the invitation of President William McKinley.

---

[96] Sherr, *Failure Is Impossible*, p. xiii.

CHAPTER NINE

Martin Luther King Jr.

Inspired a Nation by Sharing His Dream

He was only allotted eight minutes to speak.

Knowing that probably would not be enough time to say what he needed to say, he worked diligently through the night in his room in the historic Willard Hotel, finishing his manuscript at about 4:00 a.m. on August 28, 1963—the day of the historical March on Washington.

Some 250,000 people—black, white, young, old—from around the nation had arrived in Washington, D.C, by bus, train, plane and automobile for what would be known as the largest Civil Rights event in our nation's history.

The stage for the numerous speakers and performers was in the shadow of the Lincoln Memorial. President John F. Kennedy, who supported the movement, had elected not to attend the event, expressing concern that if the march became violent it would be seen as a threat and give members of Congress a reason to be against the bill. Originally, there had been plans to disrupt the Capitol with massive civil disobedience. But Kennedy had warned, "We want success in Congress, not just a big show at the Capitol."[97]

---

[97] Kennedy, qtd. in Thomas Siebold, ed., *Martin Luther King Jr.* (San Diego, CA: Greenhaven Press, 2000), pp.144-145.

There were many luminaries present, the most popular and respected movie stars like Charlton Heston, Sidney Poitier, and Marlon Brando and performers like Joan Baez and gospel-singer Mahalia Jackson.

The crowd stretched out in front of the Lincoln Memorial along the rectangular reflecting pool and far beyond. It was a fairly typical late summer day in Washington, sunny, hot, and humid. Camilla Williams sang the "Star Spangled Banner" at 1:30 p.m. and was followed by speaker after speaker, along with several other singers on the program. By about 3 p.m. the crowd had grown restless. They were all waiting to hear one man, the last speaker of the day, Martin Luther King Jr.

King was introduced by the very dignified A. Philip Randolph, the man who had first conceived of the March on Washington. He fired up the crowd when he called Martin Luther King Jr. "the moral leader of the nation," to thunderous cheers and shout of King's name as he made his way to the podium.[98]

Martin Luther King, Jr. Aug 1963

The symbolism of the setting could not have been more dramatic or more fitting. The backdrop of the imposing Lincoln Memorial was magnificent. The richness of standing and speaking to this huge crowd in front of the majestic statue of Lincoln—the president who exactly 100 years before had issued the

---

[98] Stephen B. Oates, *Let the Trumpet Sound: A Life of Martin Luther King, Jr.* (New York: Harper Perennial, 1994), p. 258.

Emancipation Proclamation and freed the slaves—could not have been cast better by a Hollywood movie producer.

The words and phrases King used in his message came from the Emancipation Proclamation, the Bible, the Constitution, the Declaration of Independence, the Gettysburg Address, and the patriotic song, "My Country, 'Tis of Thee."

King began reading his speech manuscript. As he opened his speech he referred to Lincoln:

> A great American in whose symbolic shadow we stand today signed the Emancipation Proclamation. This momentous decree came as a great beacon light of hope to millions of Negro slaves who had been seared in flames of withering injustice. But 100 years later, the Negro is still not free. One hundred years later, the life of the Negro is still sadly crippled by the manacles of segregation and the chains of discrimination. One hundred years later, the Negro lives on a lonely island of poverty in the midst of a vast ocean of material prosperity. One hundred years later, the Negro is still languishing in the corners of American society and finds himself an exile in his own land. So we've come here today to dramatize a shameful condition.
>
> In a sense we've come to our nation's Capital to cash a check. When the architects of our republic wrote the magnificent words of the Constitution and the Declaration of Independence, they were signing a promissory note to which every American was to fall heir. This note was a promise that all men, yes, black men as well as white men, would be guaranteed the unalienable rights of liberty and the pursuit of happiness.

It is obvious today that America has defaulted on this promissory note insofar as her citizens of color are concerned. Instead of honoring this sacred obligation, America has given the Negro people a bad check; a check which has come back marked "insufficient funds." But we refuse to believe that the bank of justice is bankrupt. . . . So we've come to cash this check—a check that will give us upon demand the riches of freedom and the security of justice.[99]

He then warned the audience that there had to be a sense of urgency in getting this problem resolved, that there was no time for gradualism: "Now is the time to make real the promises of democracy. Now is the time to rise from the dark and desolate valley of segregation to the sunlit path of racial justice. Now is the time to lift our nation from the quicksand of racial injustice to the solid rock of brotherhood."[100]

King went on to exhort those involved in the struggle for civil rights to abstain from violence and to avoid doing wrong. He told them to avoid bitterness and hatred: "We must forever conduct our struggles on the high plane of dignity and discipline. We must not allow our creative protest to degenerate into physical violence. Again and again we must rise to the majestic heights of meeting physical force with soul force."[101]

He then proceeded to answer the question often posed to those in the civil rights movement about when they would be satisfied. His response was powerful:

We can never be satisfied as long as the Negro is the victim of the unspeakable horrors of police brutality. We

---

[99] King, qtd. in Oates, *Let the Trumpet Sound*, p. 259.
[100] King, qtd. in Oates, *Let the Trumpet Sound*, p. 259.
[101] King, qtd. in Oates, *Let the Trumpet Sound*, p. 260.

can never be satisfied as long as our bodies, heavy with the fatigue of travel, cannot gain lodging in the motels of the highways and the hotels of the cities. We cannot be satisfied as long as the Negro's basic mobility is from a smaller ghetto to a larger one. We can never be satisfied as long as our children are stripped of their selfhood and robbed of their dignity by signs stating "For Whites Only." We can never be satisfied as long as a Negro in Mississippi cannot vote and a Negro in New York believes he has nothing for which to vote. No, no, we are not satisfied, and we will not be satisfied until justice rolls down like waters and righteousness like a mighty stream.[102]

King was getting a tremendous response from the crowd causing his energy and emotions to surge. He exhorted the crowd to go back to their "home states in the South, and to their slums and ghettoes in the North, and know that somehow the situation was going to change."[103]

Reflecting later on his speech, King wrote, "And, all of a sudden this thing came to me. The previous June, following a peaceful assemblage of thousands of people in downtown Detroit, Michigan, I had delivered a speech in Cobo Hall, in which I used the phrase, 'I have a dream.' I had used it many times before, and I just felt that I wanted to use it here. I don't know why. I hadn't thought about it before the speech. I used the phrase, and at that point I just turned aside from the manuscript altogether and didn't come back to it."[104]

When King starting speaking extemporaneously from his heart

---

[102] Oates, *Let the Trumpet Sound*, p. 260.

[103] Oates, *Let the Trumpet Sound*, p.260.echo it exactly

[104] Martin Luther King, Jr., *The Autobiography of Martin Luther King, Jr.*, ed. Clayborne Carson (New York: IPM, 1998), p. 223.

using his "I Have a Dream" mantra, his speech soared! The speech was elevated from a run-of-the-mill Civil Rights speech about grievances and inequities for his race into a speech that would inspire millions then and long into the future.

King exhorted his followers, saying, "Let us not wallow in the valley of despair. I say to you today, my friends: so even though we face the difficulties of today and tomorrow, I still have a dream. It is a dream deeply rooted in the American dream. I have a dream that one day this nation will rise up and live out the true meaning of its creed—we hold these truths to be self-evident that all men are created equal."[105]

He spoke of his dream that the sons of former slaves and slave owners would be able to sit together in peace and brotherhood. He also said he dreamed that even the state of Mississippi with all its oppression and injustice would become "an oasis of freedom and justice."[106]

And then came one of his most memorable and cherished remarks: "I have a dream that my four little children will one day live in a nation where they will not be judged by the color of their skin but by the content of their character."[107]

The faith he dreamed of would

> be able to transform the jangling discords of our nation into a beautiful symphony of brotherhood. With this faith we will be able to work together, to pray together, to struggle together, to go to jail together, to stand up for freedom together, knowing that we will be free one day.
>
> This will be the day; this will be the day when all of

---

[105] King, *The Autobiography*, p. 226.
[106] King, *The Autobiography*, p. 226.
[107] King, *The Autobiography*, p. 226.

God's children will be able to sing with new meaning: "My country 'tis of thee, sweet land of liberty, of thee I sing. Land where my fathers died, land of the Pilgrims' pride, from every mountainside, let freedom ring!" And If American is to be a great nation, this must become true. . . . And when this happens, when we allow freedom [to] ring, when we let it ring from every village and every hamlet, from every state and every city, we will be able to speed up that day when all of God's children, black men and white men, Jews and Gentiles, Protestants and Catholics, will be able to join hands and sing in the words of the old Negro spiritual, "Free at last, free at last. Thank God Almighty, we are free at last."[108]

As he stepped down from the platform the mood was electric. The crowd was jubilant, cheering, shouting and applauding. Ralph Abernathy grabbed him and hugged and told him that the Holy Spirit had taken hold of him in the speech. A British journalist came up to him and told him and that the speech "was the most moving and magnificent public address I have ever heard."[109] Later that afternoon at a reception at the White House witnesses recalled that President John F. Kennedy "was bubbling over with the success of the event."[110]

The March on Washington had changed the paradigm. Millions of whites had watched the massive spectacle of more than a quarter million people gathered peacefully in front of the Lincoln Memorial. The people they saw on their televisions that day were black and white, men and women, young and old. They also saw clergy, highly placed politicians, well-known movie stars and entertainers. And they saw Martin Luther King Jr. speaking as a

---

[108] King, *The Autobiography,* p. 227.
[109] Quoted in Oates, *Let the Trumpet Sound,* p. 262.
[110] Oates, *Let the Trumpet Sound,* p. 262.

statesman.

King spoke as a modern-day Lincoln as he called for a new birth of freedom and called for the nation to address and fix injustices, inequalities, and the evils of racism. His soaring speech changed the dynamics of the Civil Rights Movement on that hot August afternoon. Just as Lincoln's Emancipation Proclamation 100 years earlier had elevated the cause of the Union to a new moral high, King's "I Have a Dream" speech forever changed the dynamics of race in America.

What had prepared King for this day, this speech?

The Early Years

He was born Michael Luther King Jr. on January 15, 1929, at the family home in Atlanta, Georgia. His name would be changed to Martin rather than Michael when he was six years old.

His parents were loving, and his home life was secure and comfortable. His mother, Alberta Williams King, was a devout Christian. King said that from an early age she instilled self-respect in her children. She spent time explaining about discrimination and why it existed, telling her kids why the South was divided into "White and Colored" in restaurants, schools, housing, and so many other places. She made sure her children understood they were as good as anybody else and to never feel inferior.

His father, Martin Luther King Sr., was a strong man both physically and mentally. He had persevered to attend and complete Morehouse College in Atlanta. He was a pastor at Ebenezer Baptist Church and wielded much influence in the community. He also served as president of the NAACP in Atlanta.

The summer before King Jr. started college at Morehouse College in Atlanta, he spent his summer working on a tobacco farm in Simsbury, Connecticut, to make some money to help out with school expenses. He loved the freedom he felt in this Northern city far from the segregated South. He could eat in a fancy restaurant or attend a white church. But the reality of racial discrimination would soon rear its ugly head. He described how it felt on the train ride back to Atlanta:

> It was a bitter feeling going back to segregation. It was hard to understand why I could ride wherever I pleased on the train from New York to Washington and then had to change to a Jim Crow car at the nation's capital in order to continue the trip to Atlanta. The first time I was seated behind a curtain in a dining car, I felt as if the curtain had been dropped on my selfhood. I could never adjust to the separate waiting rooms, separate eating places, separate rest rooms, partly because the separate was always unequal, and partly because the very idea of separation did something to my sense of dignity and self-respect.[111]

Education

He entered Morehouse College at the tender age of 15 years old, having skipped the 12th grade as well as one earlier.

It was at Morehouse that he really became aware of and concerned about race. He thoroughly enjoyed his professors and the very frank classroom discussions that were held about race and economic justice.

He read Henry David Thoreau's essay "On Civil Disobedience." This was his first exposure to the theory of nonviolence. He was so fascinated by Thoreau's writing that he reread it several times.

---

[111] King, *The Autobiography*, pp. 11-12.

"I became convinced that noncooperation with evil is as much a moral obligation as is cooperation with good," King wrote in his autobiography.[112] King adopted many of teachings of Thoreau into practice in the Civil Rights Movement. Whether it was a sit-in or boycott or other protest, these were adapted from Thoreau's teaching that evil must be resisted and that no moral man can patiently adjust to injustice.

King entered Crozer Theological Seminary in Chester, Pennsylvania, in the fall of 1948. He spent much time reading many philosophers ranging from Walter Rauschenbusch to Friedrich Nietzsche, Karl Marx, and Reinhold Niebuhr to name a few.

It is important to note that he strongly rejected the teachings of Communism. His main disagreements were that it had no place for God, and it embraced ethical relativism in which almost anything was allowed, including using force, lying, and even killing because the ends justified the means. And finally, he was opposed to the political totalitarianism that made the individual always the subject of the state.

During the spring of 1950 he attended a lecture given by Howard University president, Dr. Mordecai Johnson, who had recently returned from a trip to India and was speaking on the life and teachings of Mahatma Gandhi. King was profoundly touched and inspired by the speech.

He began to read and study Gandhi's campaigns of nonviolent resistance. King wrote, "Gandhi was probably the first person in history to lift the love ethic of Jesus above mere interaction between individuals to a powerful and effective social force on a large scale. Love for Gandhi was a potent instrument for social and

---

[112] King, *The Autobiography*, p. 14.

collective transformation."[113] He believed he had found the method of social reform he had been seeking.

King left Crozer Seminary with a Bachelor of Divinity Degree and headed to Boston to begin his studies at Boston University School of Theology in September 1951.

His time at Boston University was a time of intense study, discussion, and growth. He received his Ph.D. in Systematic Theology from Boston University on June 5, 1955. His academic journey had enabled him to coalesce his belief that nonviolent resistance to oppression was one of the best weapons available in the quest for social justice and equality.

Another major dimension of the man who was to become the leader of the Civil Rights Movement matured during this period. He had finally come to grips with his faith and exactly what he believed. "I decided early to give my life to something eternal and absolute. Not to these little gods that are here today and gone tomorrow. But to God who is the same yesterday, today, and forever."[114]

Coretta Scott

While in school at Boston University he had met a number of young ladies, but none were to his particular liking. He asked a friend, Mary Powell, if she knew of any attractive young ladies that he could meet. She introduced him to Coretta Scott who was a classmate of hers at the New England Conservatory of Music. He was fortunate enough to get Coretta's telephone number. He gave her a call and she agreed to go out with him to lunch.

It didn't take long for him to become very attracted to her. This

---

[113] King, *The Autobiography*, p. 24.
[114] King, *The Autobiography*, p. 33.

young woman was smart and could talk about a variety of subjects, not just her love, music. Their conversation soon found its way to talking about racial and economic injustice.

"After an hour, my mind was made up. I said, 'So can you do something else besides sing? You've got a good mind also. You have everything I ever wanted in a woman. We ought to get married someday.'"[115] Just a year and a half later they were married in Marion, Alabama, by King's father, the Reverend Martin Luther King Sr.

Dexter Avenue Baptist Church

King's first preaching job was at Dexter Avenue Baptist Church in Montgomery, Alabama. He gave his first sermon as their minister on May 2, 1954.

While living in Montgomery and leading the Dexter Avenue Baptist Church, he became very active in the National Association for the Advancement of Colored People, better known now as the NAACP. Montgomery was the tip of the spear, the focal point in the nation, for the Civil Rights struggles in the early days of the movement.

One of the things King did his first year as pastor of Dexter Avenue Baptist Church was to form a Social and Political Action Committee within the church. Its purpose was to keep the congregation informed about what was going on socially, politically, and economically in the nation. The group was instrumental in getting church members registered to vote and become knowledgeable about the NAACP and its activities.

---

[115] King, *The Autobiography*, p. 35.

Rosa Parks and the Montgomery Bus Boycott

On December 1, 1955, Rosa Parks was riding a bus in Montgomery and was ordered to give up her seat to a white male passenger who had just boarded the bus. She was expected to move to the back of the bus to the seats where "colored people" were supposed to sit (unless a white needed a seat, in which case they were supposed to stand). Parks calmly refused to give up her seat and was ultimately arrested. Her trial was set for the following Monday, December 5.

The arrest of Parks was one of those things that at first seemed to be just another routine event. Little did anyone realize the powerful forces that would be awakened from their slumber by this seemingly small, insignificant incident.

E. D. Nixon, the signer of Park's bond, Reverend Ralph Abernathy, minister of the First Baptist Church of Montgomery, and King talked back and forth and decided that a message of protest needed to be sent and that a bus boycott would be the best way. They called for a meeting of black civic leaders and ministers for that evening. During that evening, the group agreed—the time was now to boycott the buses.

The group prepared a statement calling for all Negroes to boycott public buses on Monday, December 5, and come to a mass meeting that evening at the Holt Street Baptist Church for further instructions. Thousands of leaflets with that message were delivered by hand all over the city.

The call for a boycott was successful! Thousands of black people who normally rode buses found other ways that day to get to work, school, or wherever their destination. Some shared rides, others walked or took cabs. Some men were even seen riding mules or riding in carriages.

The Beginning of a National Movement

That afternoon several of the key organizers met prior to the evening meeting. They first decided on a name for the group, The Montgomery Improvement Association (MIA). Next came the election of officers. As soon as the floor was opened for nominations, King was nominated, seconded, and then elected by a unanimous vote.

King went home and hastily prepared for the evening meeting. He and the other organizers had agreed that if the night's event was poorly attended, the boycott would be stopped.

As he drove to the meeting at the Holt Street Church, he ran into a traffic jam several blocks away. Thousands of people were coming to the meeting. There would be a boycott!

Standing to speak that night he had no notes or manuscript and simply spoke from his heart:

> We are here this evening for serious business. We are here in a general sense because first and foremost we are American citizens and we are determined to apply our citizenship to the fullness of its meaning. We are here also because of our love of democracy, because of our deep-seated belief that democracy transformed from thin paper to thick action is the greatest form of government on earth. . . . You know, my friends, there comes a time when people get tired of being trampled over by the iron feet of oppression. . . . We are not wrong in what we are doing. If we are wrong, the Supreme Court of this nation is wrong. If we are wrong, the Constitution of the United States is wrong. If we are wrong, God Almighty is wrong. If we are wrong, Jesus of Nazareth was merely a utopian dreamer that never came down to earth. And we

are determined here in Montgomery to work and fight until justice runs down like water and righteousness like a mighty stream.[116]

Later, a vote was held on the resolution to continue their boycott until certain demands were met. It was a unanimous vote!

King would later write in his autobiography,

> I said to myself, the victory is already won, no matter how long we struggle to attain the three points of the resolution. It is a victory infinitely larger than the bus situation. The real victory was in the mass meeting, where thousands of black people stood revealed with a new sense of dignity and destiny. That night we were starting a movement that would gain national recognition; whose echoes would ring in the ears of people of every nation; a movement that would astound the oppressor, and bring new hope to the oppressed.[117]

For the next year the battle in Montgomery was waged. There was an effort to stop the transporting of Negroes by mass ticketing by the police. Those driving cars were stopped for any excuse and given tickets.

On January 30, 1956, a bomb went off on King's porch. He received the news while at church and breathlessly raced home, fearing the worse for Coretta and his baby, Yoki. Thankfully he found them unharmed.

A large crowd, hundreds of people, had gathered in his front yard, and they were angry. The police attempted to get them to disperse, but they wouldn't budge and were becoming more unruly as time

---

[116] King, *The Autobiography*, p. 60.
[117] King, *The Autobiography*, p. 62.

passed.

Finally, King came out and spoke to them saying,

> We believe in law and order. Don't get panicky. Don't
> do anything panicky at all. Don't get your weapons. He
> who lives by the sword will perish by the sword.
> Remember that is what God said. We are not advocating
> violence. We want to love our enemies. I want you to
> love our enemies. Be good to them. Love them and let
> them know you love them. I did not start this boycott. . . .
> But I want it known that if I am stopped our work will not
> stop. For what we are doing is right. What we are doing
> is just. And God is with us.[118]

His words calmed the crowd, and the people soon returned home.

In February, a Montgomery grand jury indicted King and other
MIA leaders and more than 100 others. The city said that the
blacks were violating anti-boycott laws. On March 22, 1956, King
was found guilty of leading the boycott and was fined $500 or 386
days in jail. His case was appealed.

The breakthrough came on November 13 when the United States
Supreme Court declared bus segregation laws unconstitutional. By
late December the MIA voted to end the boycott. It was a
monumental win for the Civil Rights Movement.

King's Trip to India 1959

One of the most important journeys of King's life was his visit to
India in 1959 to study the teachings of Mahatma Gandhi. Coretta
later wrote, "Martin stressed the fact that he was not traveling as a

---

[118] King, *The Autobiography*, p. 80.

tourist; instead he said 'To India, I come as a pilgrim.'"[119]

This trip had a tremendous impact on his life and his beliefs in nonviolence. He was able to travel the country extensively and meet with many proponents of Gandhi and his teaching. King was especially fascinated by the concept of *Satyagraha* which can be translated as "truth-love or love force."

He also had several discussions with the Prime Minister of India, Jawaharlal Nehru, who, while being an admirer of Gandhi and his philosophy, confessed he had not always agreed with every position of Gandhi.

King came away from the trip totally dedicated to the principles of nonviolence and with a desire to live his life as simply as possible and to avoid the trappings of a rich, highly influential leader with throngs of admirers and followers following his every word.

He also came away with a new realization that patience was a necessity in the fight for civil rights. He saw that the movement for independence of India had taken fifty years, with leaders often put in prison for ten years. Americans wanted change to come much faster. There was a sense of urgency in getting things changed now!

King stated, "I came to see for the first time that the Christian doctrine of love operating through the Gandhian method of nonviolence was one of the most potent weapons available to oppressed people in their struggle for freedom."[120]

After the March

After the heady success of the March on Washington for Jobs and

---

[119] Coretta King, qtd. in *Martin Luther King, Jr.,* ed. Siebold, p. 66.

[120] Martin Luther King, Jr. "Pilgrimage to Nonviolence" (later called "How My Mind Has Changed,") *Christian Century* 77 (April 13, 1960) p. 422.

Freedom on August 28, 1963, there would be many more setbacks, many trials and tribulations for the Civil Rights Movement.

The following month, September 15, a dynamite explosion killed four young black girls attending Sunday school at Birmingham's Sixteenth Street Baptist Church. This violence against young children horrified the nation. King would deliver the eulogy a few days later.

And then in November 1963, a huge setback occurred when President John F. Kennedy Jr., who was very supportive of the movement, was assassinated.

The summer of 1964 was a tumultuous time. Three young blacks were lynched in Mississippi, and there were riots in several cities in the North. The Republican Party's nomination of Barry Goldwater, who was seen as sympathetic toward those against the Civil Rights Movement, further widened the rift that was growing in the nation.

King would continue to lead the battle for Civil Rights for the next several years. Many important struggles would be waged: the 1965 Selma to Montgomery March and pushing for and winning the voting rights act. There were also the very disturbing, violent days of the Watts riots.

Then in March of 1968 King traveled to Memphis, Tennessee, to speak to striking sanitation workers. He led a march there that turned violent. On April 3, 1968, he gave his last address at the Bishop Charles J. Mason Temple in Memphis.

The next evening on April 4, 1968, he would be struck down and killed by an assassin's bullet.

Conclusion

Divine Providence provided a leader like Martin Luther King Jr. to lead his race and the people of this nation through those turbulent years of the Civil Rights Movement. Had there not been a leader who was totally committed to non-violence during this highly-charged time of marches, boycotts, protests, etc., our nation could have been ravaged with murder and mayhem, maybe even another civil war.

King was a voice of reason. He was a determined, effective leader who always sought to take the high road. His leadership was a steady, calming influence on the Civil Rights Movement. There were many militant black leaders like Malcolm X and groups like the Nation of Islam, the Black Panther Party, and others who openly advocated violence as a means to an end. Some wanted a race war. Thanks to King's leadership and his policies of nonviolence, that was averted.

The March on Washington in the summer of 1963 was a key, watershed event for the nation. For the first time, the movement took on an air of respectability and gravitas. It was well-organized with an extremely large number of participants—some 250,000 people. The massive assembly was filled with celebrities and people who commanded great respect. It was supported by a large group of mainline Christian churches and included more than 75,000 whites as participants.

The March received widespread coverage on national television and radio. King was pleased that millions of whites across the nation got a clear, long, look at Negroes attending the event who were well-behaved, and those watching on TV or listening on radio were impressed at hearing dynamic, well-spoken, well-informed, and thoughtful speakers.

There would be many more trying days, more months and years of pain, heartache, and struggle to gain equality, justice under the law, and economic opportunity. But King's speech at the March on

Washington was a turning point. That was the day the Civil Rights Movement came of age. It was the day the country, and the world, took notice. It was the day the pendulum began to swing in the direction of the "new birth of freedom" that Lincoln had talked about in his Gettysburg Address 100 years before.

Martin Luther King Jr., the man whose words would inspire and transform a movement, was there at the March on Washington, August 28, 1963—***When Leadership Mattered***.

Bonus Notes

- Preaching was in his blood. His father was a preacher, as were his grandfather and great grandfather. His brother and an uncle were also preachers.

- He was awarded the Nobel Peace Prize in 1964.

- In 1958 he was stabbed at a book signing in Harlem by an African American woman.

- While he studied the philosophy of Communism with great interest, he rejected it because it was too materialistic and had no place for God. It practiced relativism thus almost anything such as lying, cheating, killing was allowed to meet its ends. He also rejected the totalitarian premise that the government was superior to the individual.

CHAPTER TEN

Nehemiah

The Bible's preeminent example of leadership

It was a time of despair for Nehemiah. His nation of Israel had been defeated in war and most of its leaders were living in captivity in the conqueror's homeland.

The exiles who had returned to his homeland were in great distress, defenseless and shamed because the walls of their fathers' city, Jerusalem, had been destroyed, the gates burned and laid wasted for nearly 150 years. This was a disgrace to the Hebrews.

When Nehemiah heard a report about the desperate situation in his homeland, he wept, mourned, prayed, and fasted for many days. He cried out to God confessing the sins of the nation, including himself and his family. He felt a heavy burden to see that wall of protection rebuilt.

Serving on the staff of King Artaxerxes in Persia, Nehemiah often spent time with him. The king noticed his distress and sadness and asked him what was wrong. Before answering, Nehemiah whispered a prayer, asking God for favor with the king.

With great trepidation he told the king "the city where my fathers are buried lies in ruins, and its gates have been destroyed by fire" (Nehemiah 2:3 NIV). The king then asked him what it was he wanted.

"If it pleases the king and your servant has found favor in his sight, let him send me to the city in Judah where my fathers are buried so that I can rebuild it" (Nehemiah 2:5 NIV). The king agreed to let him go to rebuild the wall.

Nehemiah then began to demonstrate his leadership skills that would be needed to plan for and coordinate such a monumental task. He considered what was needed to make the trip to Jerusalem and what would be needed once he got there. He thought about the administrative and logistical requirements. He asked the king for letters to the rulers along the way to ensure safe passage. He also asked for a letter to the keeper of the king's forest to provide timber for him to make beams for the gates to the city.

Once he arrived at Jerusalem he went out quietly at night to assess the situation, telling no one what he was planning. This was an especially smart tactical move on his part. He inspected and analyzed the situation and formulated his plan of action before telling anyone.

Then he met with influential Jewish leaders, priests, nobles, and others who would be doing the work. He shared with them how God had burdened him regarding Jerusalem and blessed him with the favor and support of the king to see the wall rebuilt. He explained that he would personally lead the project. By the end of the briefing, the men agreed and bought in to this bold project. Some 40 key men agreed to help rebuild the wall and gates.

Nehemiah then organized the project by assigning each leader and his family to be responsible for rebuilding a specific portion of the wall and the gates. The men were given full personal responsibility for their area. There was clarity in exactly what they were expected to do and the chain of command was clearly defined.

A serious challenge to the work soon reared its ugly head.

Sanballat, governor of nearby Samaria, felt threatened by the possibility of a rejuvenated Jerusalem, believing it would alter the status quo of the region's political power and commerce.

He began to do everything possible to disrupt the project. He mocked and ridiculed the Jews at first, but having no success with that he began to threaten and intimidate them. He tried repeatedly to lure Nehemiah into a meeting with him, to harm him or at least take him away from the project so work might slow or stop.

But Nehemiah remained totally focused and refused to meet with Sanballat or to be intimidated. He demonstrated great leadership abilities as he faced dire threats of attack while he led the men working feverishly to complete the building of the wall. He implemented stringent security measures, having every man carry his weapon at all times—even when he was carrying tools or stones. He had one half of the men stand guard 24 hours a day. Because the wall was extensive and spread out, he devised a plan to quickly re-enforce any part of the wall if it came under attack. As the commander or leader he constantly kept the trumpeter at his side ready to sound the alarm if an attack came.

Nehemiah worked tirelessly, constantly checking the ongoing work and defenses. According to ancient historian Josephus, "Nehemiah himself made the rounds of the city by night, never tiring either through work or lack of food or sleep, neither of which he took for pleasure but as a necessity."[121]

Israel had plenty of men available to do the work and adequate stones, beams and supplies could certainly have been procured. What they lacked was a leader—a man with vision who could make a plan, gain the support and buy-in of others, mobilize the project, oversee it, and work tirelessly to lead it to completion.

---

[121] Josephus, *Antiquities* 11.5.8.

One man, Nehemiah, challenged the status quo. The wall that lay in ruins for nearly 150 years was rebuilt in only 52 days by a dynamic leader with the blessing of God.

Nehemiah became the catalyst that rebuilt the wall around Jerusalem in 445 B.C.—*When Leadership Mattered.*

Bonus Notes

The story of Nehemiah is one of the most complete examples of leadership I know of. Here are some of the leadership skills he demonstrated.

- He prayed. He sought divine guidance and blessing in his undertaking.

- He considered what would be required to accomplish the task.

- He obtained authority for his mission: letters from the king to have safe passage through hostile areas and to obtain timber for helping with the project.

- He personally and secretly reconnoitered the situation of the rebuilding project. He personally needed to see with his own eyes and assess it.

- He developed a comprehensive plan and brought key leaders together to brief and obtain their buy-in to the project. He also clearly let them know of his commitment.

- He, as the leader, walked around the project day and night to personally inspect and supervise the rebuilding of the wall. An old Army axiom is that "troops do well on what is inspected."

- He kept his people alert, armed, and ready to respond to any challenge.

- He would not allow himself to be deterred by any challenge, psychological warfare, or distraction. He stayed focused on the task at hand.

- He worked tirelessly and talked to and motivated his people on a regular basis.

CHAPTER ELEVEN

Steve Jobs

His vision and demand for perfection, simplicity and excellence ushered in world-changing technology

He didn't lead troops into battle. He didn't save his nation, lead a social movement, fight for equality and rights, or build a championship sports program. However, his unique leadership put the technology in our hands that changed our lives forever!

Steve Jobs, through his tenacious leadership, helped usher the world into the golden age of computers, with amazing technological advances in not only personal computers, but smart phones, iPods, iPads, entertainment, etc.

He came from humble beginnings. His natural parents, Joanne Schieble from rural Wisconsin and his father Abdulfattah "John" Jandali, of Syrian descent, gave him up for adoption. Paul and Clara Jobs, who had been unable to have children, adopted him and named their new baby Steven Paul Jobs. Before the natural mother would sign the adoption papers, the Jobs had to agree to build a fund for Steve's college education, which they did.

Bored and unchallenged with school, during his third-grade year young Steve Jobs was sent home from school several times because of his pranks.

In the fourth grade he was tested and found to be at a 10th grade level, and the decision was made for him to skip the fifth and sixth grades and go right into the seventh. While this made sense academically, socially it did not. The school was rough, and he was often bullied. By the middle of that year, he demanded that his parents get him into another school. Even though it was hard financially for his dad to buy a house in another neighborhood and school district, he did.

They moved to a three-bedroom house at 2066 Crist Drive, Los Altos, California. This home had an attached garage that would become the place where Apple would be launched.

A neighbor, Larry Lang, who was an engineer, was a big influence on young Steve Jobs and introduced him to the world of ham radios and to Heathkits, an assemble-it-yourself kit for ham radios and other electronics. This had a profound effect on Jobs who said, "It made you realize you could build and understand anything. Once you built a couple of radios, you'd see a TV in the catalogue and say, 'I can build that as well.' . . . I was very lucky, because when I was a kid both my dad and the Heathkits made me believe I could build anything." [122]

Jobs also became a member of the Hewlett-Packard Explorers Club which met weekly. At club meetings, engineers would talk to the members about projects they were working on. Jobs was fascinated. He loved it.

The club members engaged in projects and, while working on one, Jobs found he needed some parts that Hewlett Packard made. So he just picked up a phone and called the CEO, Bill Hewlett, at home. They talked for 20 minutes. Jobs not only got the parts he needed, he got a job! He worked at HP that summer on an assembly line but found his true interests were on the second floor

---

[122] Steve Jobs, qtd. in Walter Isaacson, *Steve Jobs* (New York: Simon & Schuster, 2011), p. 16.

where the engineers worked. He would go up and hang out with them every morning during their coffee break.

In his sophomore year of high school he worked in a huge electronics store where he became intimately aware of a wide variety of parts and electrical components. The store had a sprawling collection of new, used, and salvaged parts of all kinds, and he became an expert on the functions and values of the parts. He combined that expertise with a gift for haggling with customers to get the best price for the store. These skills would serve him well in the future.

Jobs did a brief stint at Reed College, a small 1,000 student liberal arts school in Portland, Oregon. The school was very expensive, and the "hippie-drug culture" was in full bloom there. Jobs took a great interest in Eastern spirituality, particularly Zen Buddhism. While there, he used LSD, became a vegetarian, and quickly became disillusioned with having to attend classes that didn't interest him. He finally dropped out of school. However, he stayed in the area and continued to monitor classes that aligned with his interests. He loved learning; he just didn't want to waste his time with classes he didn't find useful.

One class he attended was a calligraphy course, which intrigued him. This particular class would have a huge influence on the products he would produce. He later said, "If I had never dropped in on that single course in college, the Mac would never have had multiple typefaces or proportionally spaced fonts. And since Windows just copied the Mac, it's likely that no personal computers would have them."[123]

After hanging around Reed College for about 18 months he returned home to live with his parents. He quickly found a job as a

---

[123] Steve Jobs, qtd. in Walter Isaacson, *Steve Jobs*, p. 41.

technician with the video game-maker Atari, where he made $5 per hour.

Trip to India

Once he had saved enough money, he quit his job and traveled to India on a spiritual quest. During his seven months there he became very sick with dysentery and fever. His weight dropped from 160 to 120 lbs. in just a week or so. His study and practice of Zen Buddhism became an influential part of his life from this time on.

He returned home in early 1975. He had shaved his head, was wearing a flowing cotton robe, and was deeply tanned. When his parents went to pick him up at the airport they walked past him several times without recognizing him. He looked like a Hare Krishna follower.

He soon returned to work at Atari. A few months later Nolan Bushnell, founder of Atari, called Jobs in and asked him to develop a single-player version of Pong. Bushnell knew Jobs wasn't a great engineer but suspected that he would entice his friend Steve Wozniak, a fantastic engineer, into the effort. He did. In an effort that could have taken months, Wozniak and Jobs completed it in four days.

The Birth of Apple

Wozniak was the real genius who figured out how to make a machine that could type characters on a keyboard and have them show up on a computer screen. Jobs was intrigued. He would continually ask Wozniak questions about the possibilities of what the machine could do, such as whether or not it could ever be networked and could possibly store memory.

Wozniak was content to attend Homebrew Computer Club

meetings and share all his findings and knowledge with the other computer geeks for free. Jobs however, had other ideas. He convinced him to quit giving away copies of his schematics and challenged him with the idea that they could sell them and make some money.

Jobs worked out a plan to have someone at Atari draw circuit boards and print up about 50 for him. It would cost $1,000 plus a fee for the designer. They could sell them for $40 each and make a profit of $700. Wozniak was very doubtful that they would be able to sell them all and make their money back. Jobs convinced him that even if they didn't make money, they could have fun, and they would have their own company.

To raise enough working capital, Jobs sold his Volkswagen bus for $1,500 and Wozniak sold his HP 65 calculator. Jobs ended up having to pay for half the repairs needed on the bus within two weeks, and Wozniak got stiffed for half of his selling price of $500 for the calculator. So now, they now had only about $1,300 to start their company. They bandied about a number of possible names for the company, and finally settled on Apple Computer.

On April 1, 1976, Jobs (now 21 years old), Wozniak, and Ron Wayne met together to draw up a partnership agreement to form their company, Apple Computer. The shares were split 45-45-10, with Wayne being the chairman and a 10% partner who would be there to arbitrate and serve as a tie-breaker on decisions if the need arose.

However, Wayne got a severe case of cold feet and decided to pull out of the agreement completely when he saw the money that Jobs was seeking to borrow. (See Bonus Notes at end of this chapter to see what this decision ultimately cost him).

Jobs and Wozniak made a presentation to the Homebrew

Computer Club soon after forming their company. Wozniak demonstrated the new crude Apple computer followed by Jobs who tried to sell the group on the amazing technological advances of the computer. Almost to a person they were not impressed! However, one person, Paul Terrell, a computer store owner was. They talked with him and gave him a personal demonstration of the computer. As he left he gave Jobs his business card and told him to stay in touch.

Jobs' version of staying in touch meant he was at Terrell's store the next day. Jobs did such a good job convincing him of the value of the product that Terrell ordered 50 computers. The kicker was he didn't just want the circuit board that Jobs was pitching; he wanted fully assembled computers for which he agreed to pay $500 for each. When Jobs called Wozniak and told him the news about the sale, Wozniak was shocked!

Jobs then set about to borrow the $15,000 they would need for parts in order to fill this initial order for 50 computers. After several unproductive efforts to secure the money or parts, Cramer Electronics, after confirming that Jobs and Wozniak really did have a $25,000 order, agreed to front them the parts on 30 days credit.

The miracle of the birth of Apple Computer had happened. Jobs began to build a team of helpers to assemble computers in the garage of his parents' home in Los Altos, California. Aside from Jobs and Wozniak, they recruited Daniel Kottke, his former girlfriend (Elizabeth), and Jobs' sister, Patty, who was pregnant.

When the crew had assembled their first dozen computers, Jobs took them over to Terrell to inspect. Terrell was not pleased with what he saw. There was no keyboard, power supply, monitor, or case. He had expected a more finished product. There was a short standoff but Jobs convinced him to take delivery and pay. Within a month all 50 had been delivered and they had enough money and parts to build another 50 and sell them at a good profit to their friends and fellow computer hobbyists at the Homebrew Club. They soon were building another 100 units to sell to commercial businesses. Jobs convinced Wozniak that they should build in a good profit margin so they raised the price by 33% to $666.66 per unit. (They were not aware of the negative Biblical connotations of the number 666.)

While attending a computer festival in Atlantic City, New Jersey, and looking at everything the competition had, Jobs decided that their next Apple computer must be totally self-contained with everything needed including the monitor, keyboard, and power source. It also must look good, not like the scruffy-looking contraption they were currently making. He figured if it could be convenient and easy to understand, many, many, more people would be willing to buy one, not just computer geeks. As we all know now—he was right!

Apple II is launched

Jobs knew that to produce their next generation computer, the Apple II, they needed some serious capital. Many new improvements were required, including a sleek plastic case. Jobs also wanted a power source that did not require a fan—he didn't like the noise. He figured it would take at least $200,000 or more to launch the product.

Jobs approached his old boss at Atari, Nolan Bushnell, about investing in the company. He didn't bite, but he recommended Jobs see Don Valentine, a successful former marketing manager at National Semiconductor, who was now a venture capitalist. Valentine could not be convinced to invest either, but Jobs asked him for three recommendations of people who might be willing to help. One of the three names he gave him was Mike Markkula, already retired from his positions at Fairchild and Intel and a self-made multi-millionaire from his investments.

Markkula was convinced and invested $250,000 into Apple for one third equity in the company. Jobs, Wozniak and Markkula would each own 26% of the stock which left some for future investors. Markkula would be an integral part of Apple for the next two decades.

The company's sales with the Apple II took off. By their third year the sales for Apple computers was an astronomical $200 million!

On Dec. 12, 1980, Apple went public and raised $110 million in its initial public offering—one of the largest ever, at that time. Jobs was now a very, very, wealthy young man worth $256 million. It is interesting to note that on that first day 40 Apple employees became instant millionaires.[124] Within just two years the company's annual revenues were an unbelievable $1 billion.

The next several years was a time of incredible growth and development for Apple. While Jobs would have loved to run the company, he recognized he was a little too rough around the edges, and too impulsive, to effectively lead the company as CEO. In 1983 Jobs successfully lured a top CEO, John Sculley, from his helm at Pepsico, Inc. to serve as Apple's CEO. During the courtship and the early days, the two were enamored with each other—like they were kindred spirits. But over time friction developed between their contrasting core beliefs in how to treat people and run a business.

Jobs was all about the product and not at all concerned about the people. He continuously berated his people, usually chastising in

---

[124] Applemuseum.bott.org.

front of the team or at a staff meeting. He could be utterly obnoxious and often downright cruel in his comments. Sculley, in contrast, cared deeply about the people and how they were treated. As CEO, he was the one who had to deal with the emotional and professional wreckage that Jobs left lying around. With their greatly contrasting views on how to run a company and how to treat people, problems were sure to arise.

Kicked Out of Apple

Members of the Board finally came to the point they could no longer accept Jobs' rude and abrasive treatment of employees. They told Sculley he had to exercise more control over Jobs and lead the company. In May of 1985 Sculley and Jobs clashed. Jobs was aghast that they wanted him to step down from division head of Macintosh, thus relinquishing any operational control, to take over a small team and become a product visionary.

On May 28 Sculley, with the support of the Board, told Jobs that he wanted him out! The company that Jobs and Wozniak had formed almost 10 years before was now kicking him out. This was painfully hard for Jobs to accept.

Internecine warfare raged over the next several months. Jobs waged guerilla warfare against Sculley and the Board, trying to get Sculley fired and get himself back in power. It didn't work. Sculley stood firm.

The next year Jobs founded a new computer company, NeXT Computer. That same year, 1986, he also purchased Pixar from George Lucas for $10 million.

Meanwhile Apple and IBM Corp. developed an alliance to make a new personal computer microprocessor. By July 1993 Apple reported a quarterly loss of $188 million. Sculley would be replaced by Michael Spindler as chairman.

The next two years Apple struggled for footing as they introduced the Power Macintosh and decided to license their software and allow other companies to clone the Mac.

In 1996 Apple bought NeXT for $430 million. Steve Jobs was reappointed to the Apple Board of Directors and was named an advisor to Apple and its chairman and CEO, Gilbert Amelio. Bringing Jobs back "was an act of desperation on Apple's part. Because they had failed to develop a next-generation Macintosh operating system, the firm's share of the PC market had dropped to just 5.3 percent, and they hoped Jobs could help turn the company around."[125]

Back in the Saddle Again at Apple

The next year (1997) Jobs became the "interim CEO" as Gil Amelio was shoved out. One of the first things Jobs did was quickly end Mac clones. Some other actions he took were to make a deal with Microsoft to help ensure Apple's survival. Microsoft invested $150 million in Apple for a non-voting minority stake in the company. Jobs also had a new G3 PowerPC microprocessor installed in all Apple computers making them faster than the competition's PCs.

By 1998, under Job's leadership, Apple was once again a profitable corporation with sales of $5.9 billion. In 2000 Apple made Jobs the CEO, taking away the "interim" title.

Against all odds, Steve Jobs pulled the company he founded and loved back from the brink. Apple once again was healthy and churning out the kind of breakthrough products that made the

---

[125] "Steve Jobs: An Extraordinary Career," *Entrepreneur*. Technology editor Jason Fell and research editor Carolyn Sun contributed to this article.

Apple name synonymous with innovation.

Over the next decade, the company produced a series of revolutionary products including the iPod portable digital audio player in 2001, the Apple iTunes Store in 2003, the iPhone handset in 2007, and the iPad tablet computer in 2010. These products were simple and easy to use and became widely popular throughout the world.

Why Include Steve Jobs in a Book about Leadership?

To be sure, he was a visionary. He could envision what he wanted his products, i.e., iPhones, computers, etc., to do. He wanted to make computers that could help average people manage their business, home, and personal affairs. He wanted his products to be simple and easy to use and understand. He demanded perfection. Every device he developed had to look exactly right, feel right, and operate flawlessly.

Malcom Gladwell writing a piece in *The New Yorker* in 2011 proposed that the real genius of Steve Jobs was that he was an amazing tweaker. He wrote, "The great accomplishment of Jobs' life is how effectively he put his idiosyncrasies—his petulance, his narcissism, and his rudeness—in the service of perfection." He said that Jobs' credo was "I'll know it when I see it." [126]

Examples of his leadership

One of my favorite examples of his leadership was shown when Jobs wanted a very special strong glass for the screen of the new Apple iPhone. He had been told he should talk to the young CEO of Corning Glass, Wendell Weeks. Jobs met with him and told

---

[126] Malcolm Gladwell, "The Tweaker: The Real Genius of Steve Jobs," *The New Yorker*, November 14, 2011.

him the type of glass he was seeking for the iPhone.

Weeks described a glass that Corning had made in the past but had discontinued because there was no market for it. Jobs then proceeded to start explaining to Weeks how glass was made. Weeks, who knew far more about glass than Jobs, said, "Can you shut up . . . and let me teach you some science?"[127]   His lecture on the "gorilla glass" that his company had discontinued won Jobs over completely.

Jobs told Weeks he needed as much of the gorilla glass as they could make in six months for the screen on the Apple iPhone. Weeks bluntly told him, "We don't have the capacity. . . . None of our plants make the glass now," but Jobs told Weeks, "Don't be afraid."[128]

Weeks "tried to explain that a false sense of confidence would not overcome engineering challenges, but that was a premise that Jobs had repeatedly shown he didn't accept. He [Jobs] stared at Weeks unblinking. 'Yes, you can do it,' he said. 'Get your mind around it. You can do it.'"[129]

Later Weeks would recount this story and how they actually produced a glass that had never been made and got it done in under six months. Weeks said, "We put our best scientists and engineers on it, and we just made it work."[130] Jobs sent Weeks a memo on the day that the iPhone came out and said, "We couldn't have done it without you." That memo was framed and put on Weeks' wall. [131]

To me this story exemplifies one of Job's greatest abilities—

---

[127] Isaacson, *Steve Jobs*, p. 471.
[128] Isaacson, *Steve Jobs*, p. 471.
[129] Isaacson, *Steve Jobs*, p. 472.
[130] Weeks, qtd. in Isaacson, *Steve Jobs*, p. 472.
[131] Isaacson, *Steve Jobs*, pp. 472.

getting people to accomplish more than they thought was possible.

Another such instance occurred when the Macintosh was being developed. Jobs was not happy with how long it was taking for the computer to boot up. The engineer, Larry Kenyon, explained to Jobs all the reasons why it just wasn't possible to boot up faster.

Jobs then challenged him saying, "If it would save a person's life, could you find a way to shave 10 seconds off the boot time?"[132] The engineer acknowledged that he probably could. Jobs then went to a whiteboard and demonstrated to him that if five million people were using the Mac and it took an extra 10 seconds for each of them to turn on their computer every day, that added up to 300 million hours or so per year—the equivalent of 100 lifetimes in a year. His challenge worked. "After a few weeks Kenyon had the machine booting up 28 seconds faster!"[133]

Demanding Perfection and Instilling Pride in Employees for Their Excellence!

When the design for the box that the Macintosh would go in was being developed, Jobs would not allow anything less than perfection. He knew that people judged books by their cover and he wanted the "cover" or box for the Mac to be flawless. "He got the guys to redo it fifty times," recounted Alain Rossman.[134] Even though he knew the box would be thrown into the trash as soon as the computer was taken out, he still demanded that it be perfect. For Jobs every detail was critical in making the Macintosh amazing.

---

[132] Jobs, qtd. in Walter Isaacson, "The Real Leadership Lessons of Steve Jobs," *Harvard Business Review*, April 2012.

[133] Walter Isaacson, "The Real Leadership Lessons of Steve Jobs," *Harvard Business Review*, April 2012.

[134] Rossman, qtd. in Isaacson, *Steve Jobs*, p. 134.

When the design was finally completed he called the team together for a ceremony. He said "Real artists sign their work," he said.[135] He got out a sheet of drafting paper and a Sharpie pen and had everyone come and sign their names. He was the last of the 46 people present to come up and sign the paper. He wrote his name in lower case in the center of the page with a great flourish. The names would be engraved on the inside of computer. No one would ever see them, except possibly someone repairing the computer; but the fact that they were there sent a big message to the team. Then he toasted the team with champagne. One of the team members remarked, "With moments like this, he got us seeing our work as art."[136]

Breakthrough Innovation—Pushing the Envelope

The most far-reaching success for Jobs was probably the introduction of the iPhone. It combined three revolutionary

products in one device. Job's own words in January 2007 at the launch of the iPhone at Macworld in San Francisco summed it up best:

"Every once in a while a revolutionary product comes along which changes everything. . . . Today we're introducing three

Steve Jobs at Macworld 2007

revolutionary products of this class. The first is a widescreen iPod with touch controls. The second is a revolutionary mobile phone. And the third is a breakthrough Internet communications device."

---

[135] Job, qtd. in Isaacson, *Steve Jobs*, p. 134.
[136] Isaacson, *Steve Jobs*, p. 134.

He repeated the list for emphasis, then asked, "Are you getting it? These are not three separate devices, this is one device and we are calling it iPhone."[137]

Vision, Adaptability, Tenacity

Jobs exhibited these traits when he decided that he wanted to open Apple retail stores in high-traffic, high-end malls—something no other computer company had ever done. He wanted to control every aspect of his Apple products from design, production, and marketing to sales and service. He loathed the idea that his Apple products might sit on a shelf in a big box store between his competitors' products, being sold by a clerk who had no real affinity or appreciation of Apple and could only read or recite the spec sheets from each product.

His board wasn't enamored with the idea of opening Apple retail stores. The one exception was Millard "Mickey" Drexler, CEO of Gap, who shared Job's passion for controlling the product from start to finish. He advised Jobs to build a prototype store and then study, analyze, and tweak it until it was just like he wanted it. So a store was procured, outfitted, staffed and it became the working laboratory for the development of future Apple stores.

He made Drexler, Larry Ellison, and other trusted business friends come and visit the store often and eagerly sought their advice on how to improve it. Jobs was continually looking for ways to streamline every aspect of the customer's interaction. He also spent hours and hours mulling over every aesthetic aspect of the store: layout, colors, textures, every visual and physical aspect of the store.

Toward the end of the process one of Job's advisors, Ron Johnson,

---

[137] Jobs, qtd. in Isaacson, *Steve Jobs*, p. 465.

an expert in merchandizing and launching distinctive products, delivered a troubling recommendation to Jobs. Johnson woke up in the middle of the night and realized they had gotten something wrong. It came to him that instead of organizing the store around the main Apple product lines, they should try organizing around things that people might want to do, such as a "go to a movie" bay where they could learn how to import videos from their Mac or video camera and edit them. He told Jobs they needed to reconfigure the stores.

Jobs was not happy! He said, "Do you know what a big change this is? I've worked my a** off on this store for six months, and now you want to change everything!" They drove the short drive over to the store in complete silence. When they arrived and went into a meeting, Jobs started by saying, "Ron thinks we've got it all wrong. He thinks it should be organized not around products but instead around what people do. . . And you know, he's right."[138]

Jobs had completely processed the recommendation in his mind on the ride over, swallowed his resentment, and come to the conclusion that even though it would delay the rollout by three or four months, it was the right thing to do. "We've only got one chance to get it right," Jobs said. [139] Apparently they did get it right. That fact was proven as Apple stores averaged 5,400 visitors a week by 2004 compared to 250 per week for Gateway stores. The stores did $1.2 billion in sales setting a record in the retail industry for reaching the billion dollar level.

When writing this chapter I visited a local Apple store just to get an updated, firsthand look at their operation. It was located in an upscale mall in Norfolk, Virginia. While customer traffic seemed to be extremely light throughout the mall that morning, the one

---

[138] Jobs, qtd. in Isaacson, *Steve Jobs*, p. 373.
[139] Jobs, qtd. in Isaacson, *Steve Jobs* p. 373.

exception was the Apple store.

A quick look into the bright, airy, simplistic, store revealed nearly 70 customers. They were a microcosm of America: young, old, black, white, Asian, Hispanic and other ethnicities. Each customer was met at the entrance (there is only one entrance) by a traffic manager, "Teresa" in my case, who answers questions and directs customers to the appropriate area of the store. Then I was very courteously handed off to a sales representative, "Heather", who showed me every product line and expertly explained capabilities and comparisons. Both young women loved the company, loved their jobs, and were amazingly professional in their work. It appeared to me that Steve Jobs had been absolutely right on his concept of Apple stores.

Focus

In an article in the *Harvard Business Review* Walter Isaacson revealed what he believed was the real genius, the real leadership lessons that Jobs demonstrated.

The first thing Isaacson listed about Jobs was his amazing ability to focus on what really mattered. An illustration of Jobs' brilliance is shown in the story Isaacson tells about when Jobs returned to Apple in 1997. He described how Jobs dutifully went to several weeks of briefings about products review. Finally, he had all he could stand.

"Stop! This is crazy," he said. He proceeded to grab a magic marker and walk to a white board where he drew a 2 x 2 grid and said, "Here is what we need." He wrote "Consumer" and "Pro" at the top of the board—then "desktop" and "portable" beneath them. He told the team to focus on four great products—one for each quadrant. "All others should be cancelled!" There was a stunned silence in the room. However, by getting Apple to focus on making four computers, he saved the company.[140]

Under Jobs' leadership the company went from 350 products to 10 in just two years. At a Macworld Developers Conference in 1997 he explained, "When you think about focusing, you think, 'Well, focusing is about saying yes.' No! Focusing is about saying no." Jobs was after extraordinary results and he knew there was only one way to get there. Jobs was a "no" man."[141]

Jobs had the ability to look ahead and not be limited to current ways of doing things. Once at a retreat a team member asked if we should do some market research to see what the customers wanted. Jobs responded, "No, because customers don't know what they want until we've shown them."[142] He repeated a phrase attributed to Henry Ford, "If I had asked customers what they wanted, they would have told me, 'a faster horse.'"

Conclusion

Steve Jobs changed the way the world communicates, does business, teaches, and conducts sales. His products have even changed how and where people work. Jeanette Mulvey, writing in *Business News Daily*, said, "People are no longer strictly bound to the physical setting of their office – but may now work from home in another city, state or even country."[143]

She also noted that his products have changed how we travel for

---

[140] Isaacson, "The Real Leadership Lessons of Steve Jobs," April 2012.

[141] Jobs, qtd. in Gary Keller with Jay Papasan, *The ONE Thing: The Surprisingly Simple Truth Behind Extraordinary Results* (Austin, TX: Bard Press, 2012), p. 192.

[142] Jobs, qtd. in Isaacson, *Steve Jobs*, p. 143.

[143] Jeanette Mulvey, "12 Ways Steve Jobs Changed How the World Works," *Business News Daily*, Oct. 6, 2011.

business. People no longer have to take heavy books, bulky files, or reams of paper for sales meetings or presentations.

It is amazing to note that his iPhone replaced many, many, other products or services such as GPS, maps, libraries, watches, movie guides, restaurant guides, tape recorders, cameras, video cameras, weather, news, language translators, Facetime, calculators. People can now instantly access news, sports, stocks, and weather.

IPhones have dramatically changed the lives of millions by giving them instant access to a wealth of knowledge, information, and services undreamed of just a few years ago.

His innovative products helps families and friends separated by distance stay in touch daily with apps like Facebook, Skype, twitter, and a host of others on their hand held devices, iPads or computers. Grandparents separated by hundreds, maybe thousands of miles, can now read a story to their precious grandchild every single day if they choose.

Jobs wanted simplicity in all his products. He had them made so that ordinary people could operate them intuitively—no one had to be a computer geek to understand how to do the basics. "Jobs won over an entire planet with stunning designs, technically complex and yet simple to use. The devices were remarkable, yet elegant."[144]

In this chapter I've purposely left out some of the more unpleasant facts about Steve Jobs, such as his use of drugs, poor hygiene in his early adult years, his extremely harsh and brutal, even cruel, treatment of staffers at times.

---

[144] Susan Kalla, "10 Leadership Tips from Steve Jobs" Forbes, online April 2, 2012.

Instead I chose to concentrate on the remarkable impact his leadership had on all of our lives. Whether it's where or how we work, talk to our families around the globe, pitch a sales meeting or enjoy animated movies, he made a very positive difference in our lives and the world. Steve Jobs helped build Apple into the most valuable publicly traded company in the world.

By his incredible vision, tenacity, demand for excellence, simplicity and focus he helped usher in unimaginable technological advances in the electronics industry, entertainment industry, communications, business and personal computing. Steve Jobs was there—***When Leadership Mattered***.

Bonus Notes

- When Steve Jobs took Pixar public in 1996 his 80 percent share of the first day sales was $1 Billion!

- His iTunes sold 1 million songs in the first week.

- Apple became a Fortune 500 company in seven years.

- In the third grade he set off a small explosive under the chair of his teacher. In today's zero tolerance society he would likely be expelled from the school.

- When Jobs's parents took him to Reed College in the fall of 1972 to begin his college education, he refused to let them come on campus. He would not even say good-bye to them. It was one of the very few things he ever admitted to regretting.

- When he went to Atari seeking a job he was unkempt—hair and dress disheveled—and wearing sandals. He demanded a job. He told the HR person, he not leaving until he was hired. He got hired! His supervisor would later complain that he was a hippie with body odor.

- Today, more than 700 Million iPhones are in use. It is projected by *Fortune* magazine that in a couple of years there will be one billion in use!

- Did you know that using iPhones or smartphones for making telephone calls doesn't even rank in the top 10 uses? The number one use is for texting, followed by Facebook, camera, news, shopping, and weather. Surprisingly, making telephone calls comes in at number 11 in a poll done recently in the UK by Express.

- Jobs was listed as the inventor or co-inventor of 346 U.S. patents. Most of these tech patents were related to design. According to *Business Insider* Facebook is the most used app on smartphones. It is used by an astounding 81 percent of smartphone users.

- Ron Wayne who sold his 10 percent share of Apple in 1976 for $2,300 would have been worth $2.6 billion in 2010. Years later as he lived alone in his small home in Pahrump, Nevada, subsisting on his social security checks, he said he had no regrets—that he had made the right decision for him.

- As Steve Jobs lay dying, his last words were, "Oh wow. Oh wow. Oh wow," as he gazed over the shoulders of his family.

CHAPTER TWELVE

Coach John Wooden

"Greatest Coach of the Twentieth Century"

A culture is only as strong as those who inspire its people to goodness and responsible citizenship. It is remarkable how just one person can teach and inspire millions leaving a legacy that will have a lasting, positive impact on a community, a nation, or the world.

John Wooden was one such person who has inspired and motivated generations of athletes and leaders of all kinds to excellence. Of all the sports heroes and superstars who ever played or coached basketball at the highest levels, his name stands above all the rest.

Known simply as "Coach" to millions of basketball players and fans, his UCLA teams won 10 national championships including seven in a row! His teams won 19 PAC 10 conference championships. They once won 88 consecutive games. His Bruins had an incredible record of 149 wins versus 2 losses while playing at home in Pauley Pavilion Los Angeles!

Wooden is one of only two people ever elected to the Basketball Hall of Fame as both a player and a coach. Many of his admirers don't know that he was a three-time All-American as a basketball player at Purdue University.

In addition to these phenomenal accomplishments, he was also selected by both ESPN and the NCAA as the "Greatest Coach of the Twentieth Century."

But aside from all the trophies in the trophy cases, the championship banners hanging in Pauley Pavilion, and the plaques that hung on his walls, there is a much longer lasting, more enduring effect of Coach John Wooden. That is the impact he had on untold thousands of lives by his extraordinary teaching, coaching, and inspirational leadership.

Wooden taught and mentored hundreds, probably thousands, of players, coaches, and staff members, as well as many more thousands who learned from him at basketball camps and clinics or heard him speak at lectures or conferences. He inspired leaders and those who aspired to become leaders.

At a time when values, common sense, and standing for what is right was desperately needed in our country, Coach John Wooden taught and exhibited sound principles to generations of athletes and coaches.

Wooden's coaching career included the 1960s and 1970s when the American culture was in a tremendous upheaval. The country was fighting a seemingly endless war in Vietnam, and there were anti-war protests raging across the nation. Also, it was a time of great civil unrest because of strained race relations and the Civil Rights Movement. Additionally, there was a pervasive culture of permissive drug use and rebellion against society's time honored values and traditions.

It was a challenging time not only to be a college basketball coach but also a leader in any position of authority. It was in this extremely challenging, turbulent period of resistance to authority and unrest that Coach Wooden thrived.

What made Coach Wooden stand out above all the rest? Undoubtedly there were many, many, other very fine coaches during the period he coached. What made him different?

As a young man, John Wooden learned his unshakeable, bedrock foundational beliefs from his father who always stressed hard work, integrity, and faith to him.

His father, Joshua Hugh Wooden, whom the coach idolized, gave him a copy of seven principles when he was 12 years old on the day he graduated from eighth grade. His dad didn't have money to purchase a gift, so his simple gift to his son that day was "a two dollar bill, and a small card with a poem on one side and these seven rules for living on the other."[145] He said, "Son, try to live up to this."[146] John Wooden put that piece of paper in his wallet and kept it with him throughout his life.

Coach John Wooden's Seven Life Principles

1. Be true to yourself.

2. Help others.

3. Make each day your masterpiece.

4. Drink deeply from good books, especially the Bible.

5. Make friendship an art.

6. Build a shelter against a rainy day by the life you live.

7. Pray for guidance and counsel, and give thanks for your blessings each day.[147]

---

[145] Pat Williams with Jim Denney, *Coach Wooden: The 7 Principles That Shaped His Life and Will Change Yours* (Grand Rapids, MI:, Revell, 2011), p. 24.
[146] Williams with Denney, *Coach Wooden*, p. 27.
[147] Williams with Denney, *Coach Wooden*, pp. 26-27.

Bill Walton, former UCLA and NBA star whom Coach Wooden called, "the most complete player I ever had the privilege of teaching,"[148] tells two short vignettes that speak volumes about Coach Wooden and illustrate his firm adherence to foundational principles that made him successful.

The first story takes place on Walton's first day of practice at UCLA in 1970. He had wanted to play for Wooden and UCLA since he was a young boy; there was never any doubt in his mind. On that first day of practice all the players were warming up before practice at Pauley Pavilion, and Walton could hardly wait for practice to begin.

In walks Coach Wooden, 61 years old, a fairly small, old-looking man, and he calls for the new guys to come with him.

The "new guys" were a highly touted freshmen group that consisted of Walton, Jamal Wilkes, Greg Lee, Hank Babcock, Vince Carson, and Gary Franklin.

Walton thought Coach would probably take them to a side court and let them play to see what kind of game they had. Instead he took them back to the locker room. Walton then figured the coach was going to let them in on some special knowledge and insight on what it took to become a great champion at UCLA. He and the others were in for a surprise.

"Pay attention. This is how you put on your shoes and socks," Coach said to the disbelieving star athletes. He then took off his own shoes and socks and painstakingly demonstrated exactly how they were to put on their socks "so they wouldn't wrinkle, pulling them up over our toes, around the heel, and up at the ankle,

---

148 John Wooden and Don Yaeger, *A Game Plan for Life: The Power of Mentoring* (New York: Bloomsbury USA, 2009), p. 117.

smoothing them out from the bottom up along the way," Walton explained.

The coach then demonstrated in the same way, how to correctly put shoes on. He told them to tighten the laces from bottom to top making sure the shoe fit snugly, and then to double tie them so they would not come undone.

"He made the point that it was critically important that our equipment was always in perfect order and condition, and never to allow things under our control to fail," Walton recalled.

When the lecture was over the players all looked at each other in disbelief at what had just transpired. Had the smartest coach in college basketball really just taken the time to tell them how to put on their socks and shoes?

Walton then finished the story. "Coach looked at them and said, 'If your socks and shoes aren't properly fitted, your foot will slide in your shoe during practice. That will lead to blisters. If you have blisters, you won't practice. If you don't practice, you won't play. If you're not in the game it's tough to be successful.' "

After a time Walton realized that Coach was giving them a foundation to build on. "The lesson was simple: You can only be successful at the big things if you do the little things right," Walton summarized. "Through years of observing him and his meticulous attention to detail, I realized that his teaching was timeless. Everything went back to the foundation, the building blocks, the structure upon which success is built." [149]

The other story Walton relates is especially poignant in this day and time when star athletes are coddled and treated like royalty,

---

[149] The story is recounted in Wooden and Yaeger, *A Game Plan for Life*, pp. 120-121.

even as young as high school.

The incident took place during Walton's senior year at UCLA on photo day. Walton showed up with long hair and a beard. He knew that Coach Wooden had rules against each, but he felt that Coach Wooden's rules were outdated, and so he decided to challenge him on it.

"When I explained my reasoning, Coach gave me a look that was more sympathetic than stern. Then he said, 'Bill, I acknowledge that you have a right to disagree with my rules. But I'm the coach here, and we're sure going to miss you.' With that said he walked away." Walton was unbelieving since he had been MVP for the past two years on a team that was the national champions.

Walton wrote, "Would he really dismiss me over a silly rule? I wasn't about to find out. I grabbed a bicycle and raced to the nearest barbershop and got my hair cut and beard shaved. I was back in what seemed like 15 minutes."

Years later, Walton asked Coach if he really would have dismissed him over challenging him on this rule. Coach Wooden replied in his simple straightforward way, "All that matters Bill, is that at that moment you believed that I would."[150]

The best description of what it was like to play for Coach Wooden comes from Swen Nater, a former player for Coach at UCLA who later played 12 years of professional basketball. Interestingly, Nater was told when he was recruited by Wooden that he would not get much playing time but that he would be practicing every day against the best college center in the country. "He promised the experience would help me reach my potential, provided I put in

---

[150] The story is told in Wooden and Yaeger, *A Game Plan for Life,* pp. 124-125.

the effort required."[151]

> From the moment he stepped on the practice floor, he set the tone for the intensity; the meter was always pegged high, and he worked our tails off for the entire two hours. He demanded our best effort, every minute of practice. He corrected every mistake, became disgusted and impatient often, and sparingly distributed praises. Mentally, emotionally, and physically, he drove us to the brink of collapse. It seemed like nothing was ever good enough. Perfection was what he was after. He was like a drill sergeant.
>
> And it didn't stop there. He demanded impeccable class attendance, never condoned inconsiderate treatment of others, strongly addressed waste, despised the mistreatment of animals, and would not put up with inappropriate language. If he found one piece of trash in our locker room after a practice, we would hear about it at his next opportunity. He was a stickler for proper dress; even our practice shirts had to be tucked in with a minimum degree of slack allowed. Any player who tried to get away with anything was immediately spotted and received a lecture. [152]

Nater goes on to say, "My personal experience confirms the effectiveness of Coach Wooden's principles and practices. In the history of professional basketball, no one who had failed to play

---

[151] Swen Nater and Ronald Gallimore, *You Haven't Taught Until They Have Learned: John Wooden's Teaching Principles and Practices* (Morgantown, WV: Fitness Information Technology, 2006), p. 2.
[152] Swen Nater & Ronald Gallimore, You Haven't Taught Until They Have Learned: John Wooden's Teaching Principles and Practices, p. 18.

high school basketball or start in a major college basketball game was ever drafted in the first round of the NBA and ABA until I was fortunate enough to be chosen." [153]

Wooden was never just about teaching his team basketball—he was teaching them about life. Coach required common courtesy, decency, proper appearance, punctuality, and 100 percent effort. He set high standards for his players and strictly enforced them.

Coach would absolutely not tolerate profanity. If he heard profanity at practice, he would dismiss the player for the day. All the players knew that if they didn't practice, they would not play in games. If he observed a player using profanity during a game, the player would be benched. It didn't take long for them to get the message.

Unlike so many of today's coaches, Wooden himself never cursed. One of his players, when asked if Coach ever cursed said, "'Goodness gracious, sakes alive' is profanity for the coach."[154]

He made his players clean up locker rooms at home and especially when they were the visiting team. There would be no soap, trash, etc., left lying around, ever.

Coach didn't allow flashiness, today better known as "taunting or celebrating." When Walt Hazzard, a future consensus All-American, was a sophomore, Coach had to bench him two games in a row because, "It wasn't easy to get Walt to give up some of his playground habits." Wooden told Hazzard that he had three choices, "play the game my way, sit and not play, or go someplace else."

---

[153] Swen Nater & Ronald Gallimore, You Haven't Taught Until They Have Learned: John Wooden's Teaching Principles and Practices, p. 19.
[154] John Wooden and Jay Carty, *Coach Wooden: One-on-One* (Ventura, CA: Regal Books, 2003), p. 47.

Wooden explained that using the bench was his most effective tool to make individuals play as team members and do what was best for the team. As a result of having to bench some of his players they lost a few games, but that "developed character in the lives of many young men. We won more championships than any other team ever has but, more important, we developed champions on and off the court,"[155] Wooden said.

He always trained his players to be self-sufficient and confident, to not look to the bench for guidance. He trained them not to expect timeouts from the coach. He taught them to come on the floor extremely prepared but never cocky.

Wooden taught his players that they had to concentrate and work hard in three areas of their lives to be successful. He expected their priorities to be 1) their studies, 2) basketball, and 3) their social lives.

As a result of his teaching, most of his players graduated and succeeded in their studies, on the court, and in their lives.

His coaching, teaching and mentoring has had a profound effect on college and professional basketball for decades (with many more to come). But those benefiting from his teaching weren't just basketball players and coaches, but players and coaches from most every sport.

Additionally, he mentored many who study the art of leadership including John Maxwell, the top leadership teacher/lecturer in the nation.

A short list of some of the people he influenced directly reads like a "Who's Who" list in American sports: Duke University basketball coach Mike Kryzyzewski; University of North Carolina

---

[155] Wooden and Carty, *Coach Wooden: One-on-One*, p. 79.

coach Roy Williams; former Indianapolis Colts head coach, Tony Dungy; University of Memphis, basketball coach, Tubby Smith; star college and professional player and television announcer, Bill Walton; athletic director and former football coach at Nebraska, Tom Osborne; head basketball coach at Butler University, Brad Stevens; prominent college and professional football coach and

now motivational speaker, Lou Holtz; former head coach of three NFL teams, Dick Vermeil; and Kareem Abdul-Jabbar, a six-time NBA Most Valuable Player, to name just a few.

He inspired thousands then, and now, with his principles of fairness, decency, hard work, self-discipline, and belief in God. Through the men and women he mentored who are now in coaching and leadership positions, and through the many books that he wrote and that have been written about him, he will

Coach John Wooden on his 96th birthday, Oct. 14, 2006

continue to be a force of sound leadership and wisdom for many, many years to come.

John Wooden, the "greatest coach of the twentieth Century" was there—***When Leadership Mattered.***

Bonus Notes

- John Wooden's life was providentially spared on two occasions. In 1944 he had orders to board the U.S.S. Franklin, but back surgery prevented him from going. The man who took his place was killed when a Japanese kamikaze plane crashed into the spot where Wooden would have been.

- Another time, because of a conflict, he cancelled and rescheduled the flight he would usually take from Atlanta to Raleigh to attend the Campbell College basketball school. The flight he was originally to be on crashed, killing all aboard.

- One of the accomplishments Wooden was most proud of was being awarded the Big 10 Medal for Academic Achievement. This award was given to the graduating athlete with the highest G.P.A.

- The coaching job at U.C.L.A. was actually his second choice. His first choice was Minnesota, but the offer got delayed because of weather and he accepted the U.C.L.A. offer.

- Wooden accepted his first honorary degree from Campbell College in May, 1973. He accepted it because of his great respect for Campbell President Norman A. Wiggins and his love for the college.

- Largely because of his participation, the Campbell College Basketball School became the largest and most successful camp in the nation. With Wooden participating, Campbell was able to draw many of the most elite coaches and players to the school.

ACKNOWLEDGEMENTS

This book would not have been possible without the devoted support of my wife, Glenda. Her encouragement, insightful ideas and tireless editing kept me focused and on target.

Also, many thanks to my family and friends for your constant encouragement. I am indebted to you all.

ABOUT THE AUTHOR

Baxter Ennis has worked in military, academic, political, defense, and publishing positions. His wide range of experiences led him to study leadership across a variety of fields and situations.

Ennis received his bachelor's degree in history from Campbell University and his master's degree in journalism from the University of Georgia. He served twenty-one years in the US Army and retired with the rank of lieutenant colonel. While serving as the 82nd Airborne Division's Public Affairs Officer, he participated in a combat parachute jump during the Panama Invasion and also served with the Division during the First Gulf War.

After the military, Ennis led the public relations department for a major university and later started his own newspaper. He served as president of the Chesapeake Rotary Club, the Virginia Beach Forum, and chairman of the Hampton Roads Leadership Prayer Breakfast. He and his wife, Glenda, live in Chesapeake, Virginia. They have three wonderful adult children and four awesome grandchildren.

Photo Credits

Patrick Henry addressing the Virginia Assembly, March 23, 1775 by Currier & Ives. Published 1876. Library of Congress, Public Domain.

Washington Crossing the Delaware River by Emanuel Leutz. Public Domain via Wikimedia Commons.

Photo of Brigadier General Joshua Chamberlain from the Brady Collection at the National Archives. Public Domain.

Theodore Roosevelt's journal on the day both his mother and his wife died. Library of Congress via Wikimedia Commons.

Theodore Roosevelt and the Rough Riders at San Juan Hill, 1898. Public Domain, Library of Congress.

Winston Churchill "The Roaring Lion" photo by Yousuf Karsh.

William Wilberforce by K.A. Hickel, 1794. Public Domain.

Abraham Lincoln photo by Alexander Gardner. Wikimedia Commons, Public Domain.

Susan B. Anthony by GE Perine. Via Wikimedia Commons. Public Domain.

Martin Luther King, Jr. at the March on Washington, August 28, 1963. Used via Wikimedia Commons.

Steve Jobs at MacWorld 2007. From Danny Novo via Creative Commons.

Coach John Wooden's photo on his 96th birthday. Public domain. www.house.gov from Congressman Brad Sherman's office.